the NO-REGRETS GUIDE *to*
RETIREMENT

the NO-REGRETS GUIDE *to*
RETIREMENT

*How to live well, invest wisely
and make your money last*

PATRICIA HOWARD

WILEY

First published in 2021 by John Wiley & Sons Australia, Ltd

42 McDougall St, Milton Qld 4064
Office also in Melbourne

Set in 11/15pt AdobeCaslonPro by SPi Global, Chennai, India

© John Wiley & Sons Australia, Ltd 2021

The moral rights of the author have been asserted

ISBN: 978-0-730-39090-9

A catalogue record for this book is available from the National Library of Australia

Cover design by Wiley

Tables 1 and 2: © Australian Taxation Office for the Commonwealth of Australia; tables 3 and 4: © Commonwealth of Australia. Services Australia website content is licensed under a Creative Commons Attribution 3.0 Australia Licence https://creativecommons.org/licenses/by/3.0/au/.

Printed in Singapore by Markono Print Media Pte Ltd

10 9 8 7 6 5 4 3 2 1

Disclaimer
Patricia Howard holds an Australian Financial Services Licence (AFSL no. 412820). This book outlines general advice only. It should not replace individual, independent, personal financial advice.
The material in this publication is of the nature of general comment only, and does not represent professional advice. It is not intended to provide specific guidance for particular circumstances and it should not be relied on as the basis for any decision to take action or not take action on any matter which it covers. Readers should obtain professional advice where appropriate, before making any such decision. To the maximum extent permitted by law, the author and publisher disclaim all responsibility and liability to any person, arising directly or indirectly from any person taking or not taking action based on the information in this publication.

Contents

Preface

So many people enter retirement expecting the worst. They worry they won't have enough money. They worry their funds won't last as long as they do, no matter how much money they have. They worry they will miss out. That they won't be able to do all the things they've dreamed about doing in life. That they simply won't enjoy life anymore.

In writing about retirement in Australia, I wanted to write a positive, practical, uplifting book. A book to help you make the most of your financial situation, whatever that is, but more importantly a book that will hopefully change your attitude. A book that will help you plan your retirement in an optimistic way, even though I know this will be a stretch for some readers.

Throughout the book, I refer to Australia's generous welfare system and I do believe Australians are fortunate to be able to access the Age Pension. I know many will baulk at this. I can hear them grumble, 'It's impossible to make ends meet on the Australian Age Pension, so how can she call it generous?'

Let me give those comments context.

I have been blessed with the great opportunity, and challenge, of living overseas, mostly in what are referred to as 'third world' countries such as Brazil, Mexico and Kenya. I'm not really sure where the first and second worlds begin and end. That's just one of life's great puzzles, I guess. It is a term, though, that suggests these countries somehow lag behind a so-called 'first world' country like Australia.

However, I would not rush to judge any of these three countries. I certainly wouldn't call them impoverished. The standard of living for most people in these countries is very poor compared to Australia and opportunities are very much more limited. Yet the people in all three countries can teach Australians a lot about enjoying what we have here and appreciating so many things we take for granted. The fresh air they don't have in Mexico City, the clean water that is so hard to come by in Kenya and the ability to walk safely through the streets, which many in Brazil only dream of.

I do think Australia's Age Pension rate is generous and I do think people retiring in Australia have the most wonderful opportunities. So many in the world don't have access to these.

I was also fortunate enough to be born in Australia. I am very mindful never to take that for granted. If you are lucky enough to be entitled to hold an Australian passport, either by birth or by choice, you have won the global lottery. We, as a nation of people, are the big winners in this world and we should always be mindful of that.

Don't waste time wishing you had more money in super or that you owned a bigger house or lived closer to the beach.

Be present in your life. Retirement is your opportunity to chill, breathe and enjoy.

Patricia Howard

Introduction

The biggest fears most people have as they approach retirement are not having enough money saved and — regardless of how much money they have — that it won't be sufficient to get them through their retirement. That their money simply won't last as long as they do.

The challenge is to put those fears aside. Australians are fortunate to have access to a generous Age Pension, and this is a significant safety net. What's more, with good management their other assets should provide more than enough to live on.

In this book, I encourage you to be optimistic and to think through the endless options you have for making the most of your life in retirement. I present you with strategies and suggestions that will help you plan your financial retirement.

Each of the nine chapters explores an aspect of money in retirement. At the end of each chapter there's a summary of the main points in the chapter and a short activity for you to complete should you wish to develop your plan further. There is ample practical advice on how you can make the most of your financial situation and make sensible choices so you can live happily for the rest of your life.

This book will help you:

- *work out how much money you will need to live comfortably in retirement.* I will help you develop strategies for making your money last and inspire you to look outside the square. To think about where you want to live and how you want to spend the next few decades of your life. And how you can tailor those dreams to fit within your budget.

- *discover that you already have a half-a-million-dollar nest egg.* The Australian Age Pension is much the same as having half a million dollars in super. In fact, it's better. You can't lose it, it will always increase with inflation and it will last as long as you do — no matter how long you live. You'll learn about your Age Pension entitlements to ensure you make the most of them and how you can use your own savings to top up whatever pension you receive.

- *grasp the concept of making the most of your investments.* Managing significant amounts of money can be a challenging task. I'll outline the key investment choices you should consider to help you make the most of your retirement savings. Ensuring you are confident about where your money is invested is a key step for achieving financial peace of mind. And it's something that's within easy reach of every Australian in retirement.

- *see the warning signs of bad investments made to look like get-rich-quick schemes.* It's easy to get caught up in the marketing hype of investment scammers, who often target people approaching retirement. Bad investment choices can drain your savings and even leave you penniless at a time in your life when you cannot recover your lost savings.

- *find out how to live like a millionaire.* By this I mean that retirement is all about generating as much income as you can as safely as you can. Once you learn how to do this, the other challenge is to ensure you spend less than your investments generate each year. That's how millionaires live. If you learn this lesson early in retirement, you will not only live like a millionaire but you will never run out of money.

- *discover ways to boost your income.* I offer plenty of ideas on how you can boost your income in retirement, as well as how to rein in your expenditure. Simple thoughts such as making money from renting out your home to generating income from your favourite hobby. There are also tips on how to live the life you want for less. Not only will this help your finances, but it should also boost your enjoyment of life.

- *master the art of avoiding the biggest financial pitfall in retirement: family.* Giving money away to family members, or family members helping themselves to their retirement savings are the most common ways people run out of money in retirement. You can protect yourself against this while still having a loving and caring relationship with your family by putting in place some much-needed safeguards.

- *become aware of the dangers of romantic follies.* Romance-based scams don't only occur on internet dating sites. Your love life can lead you to losing money, from being on the wrong side of a property investment to losing everything in a divorce. Sadly, women seem to be more at risk than men and this book provides some useful tips on how you can safeguard your finances so you are not left alone and poor in retirement.

- *realise the importance of always having a back-up plan.* It's possible for things to go wrong financially at any stage of life. The big difference in retirement, though, is that you don't have a second chance to go back and recoup the money that you lost through a poor investment or divorce. In this book, I'll go through some of the ways you can protect yourself from life's biggest financial traps and how to get yourself back on track if things go wrong.

Don't let retirement just happen to you. Make sure it's the retirement you want — so you can sit back and enjoy every minute! Let's get started.

Chapter 1

Retirement: a good news story

For most Australians, retirement is a good news story. Regardless of where you live or how much money you have, there are some great reasons to look forward to, and embrace the idea of, not working full time anymore.

Firstly, Australia is blessed with an excellent and mostly free medical system. Yes, there is the odd waiting line and it can get frustrating from time to time, but if something were to happen to you, you would be cared for and looked after. There are also wonderful support services available to provide care for you in the comfort of your home.

There have been incredible advances in modern medicine, including how we care for older people. Once, people would retire and so mark the steady decline in health to their inevitable demise. This is no longer the case. Now, if you do suffer a serious medical problem, you will invariably stop smoking, drink less, lose weight and start exercising more regularly as part of your recovery strategy. Before long, you will be feeling better than ever. So retirement, though sometimes punctuated by bouts of poor health, is more likely to consist of sustained periods of good health. Optimism and positive thinking is the name of the game these days.

Secondly, Australia has a great sense of community. No matter who you are, where you live or how much money you have, there are plenty of things you can get involved in. Perhaps you will decide to volunteer in your local op shop or hospital, or you may set up and finance your own charity or small business. Everything is possible, no matter what your age.

Australia is also blessed with a wonderful climate. As thousands of 'grey nomads' make testament to each year, it's very easy to travel the country, stay in beautiful spots for weeks on end and pay very little for the privilege. Even if you never move beyond your own suburb, the country abounds with beautiful gardens, wildlife reserves and national parks everyone can access. A sandwich and some bottled water and the day can be spent enjoying some of the best scenery and outdoor spaces in the world. It's all there on our doorstep.

Finally, Australia has the Age Pension — a significant safety net — which ensures most Australians can fully enjoy their last years. Sure, there are always exceptions and cases of hardship, yet for most Australians who have enjoyed a life of full employment and managed to pay off their own home, financially, the situation is pretty good.

An increasing number of Australians are finding they are reaching retirement age with money in superannuation — sometimes a considerable amount — and that's a great thing. Not only does this mean true independence in your later years, it also means there is less pressure on the federal government to support Australians in their old age. So when people do need government support, there is more money available to them. And that's how it should be.

While you may have some concerns about your financial position and retiring, you should take a deep breath and relax. I truly believe retirement in Australia is a good news story.

Take time to reflect

Whether you're in retirement already or planning to retire in 10 or more years, the most important thing you can do is take time to reflect on what sort of life you want to lead in your later years.

For most people, retirement makes up the best years of their lives. For the first time in decades, they are usually free of the restraints of children and debt. These are big things in themselves. It's a time when, simply put, you have time. Time to enjoy your favourite pastimes and hobbies, time to enjoy your loved ones and be there for them in a way that wasn't possible while you were working, and time to just explore yourself and the things you really want to be involved in. Whatever this may be, it's worth taking time to think about what you want to do. As they say, you only get one chance at life.

Even if you are in your sixties when you retire, it is still quite reasonable to expect to live for another 30 or possibly 40 years. That's just about equal to your entire adult life to this point! With so much time available, you might choose to do several different things in retirement. You might, for example, choose to travel widely or start a small business in the first decade of your retirement. You might then decide to settle down and live in a cosy beach hideaway for five to 10 years. Finally, you might decide to move to a more urban location and live in a small apartment where you're close to everything and don't need to drive any more. There are lots of things you can get involved in during your retirement years. In fact, what you end up doing is largely only limited by your imagination.

It is important, though, to take time out — literally — and think about what you want to do in retirement and where your priorities lie. Is it all about being close at hand to watch your grandchildren grow up or is it about watching the sunrise from an exotic location? Or is your dream to live a quiet life where you can finally give your garden all the tender loving care it needs? Think about it. Who knows what fabulous ideas you will come up with.

Of course, I can hear you saying, 'so much depends on what I can afford; it would be different if I had unlimited amounts of money'. This is the cause of most people's fears: worrying about just how much money they will need to live out retirement, how much money they will have to spend week to week and whether their money will last. It's my hope this book will help you work through these issues and develop strategies on how you can make your money last as long as you do.

Take stock of your life

Most people think by working out the value of their home, adding to this the money they have in superannuation and guessing how much they will spend each year, they will have a realistic assumption of where they stand financially. But too often, this leads to an over-simplified result.

For a lot of people, their home is their biggest asset. So start by getting your home valued as it is important to gain an understanding of exactly how much it is worth. Then, ask yourself how well staying in your family home will fit your lifestyle as you move into retirement. People often stay in a house for sentimental reasons, which can be a big mistake. You should be looking to the future and thinking about what you really want from life. Will the house help you meet those wants? It might be that it will for the first part of your retirement. However, later on, when your children are probably well established in their own homes, you might not need so much room. It doesn't make sense to stay in a big home worth several million dollars simply because you're trying to qualify for the Age Pension. Look holistically at the life you want to lead and make decisions accordingly. The most common reason people stay in their home is so they can leave it to their children. But why not embrace the exciting possibilities retirement brings without being locked into a house where the high cost of maintenance and the time taken to keep it up to scratch stop you from enjoying your life?

People often stay in a house for sentimental reasons, which can be a big mistake.

You may also have assets you haven't thought about. A holiday home or an investment property? A caravan or a boat? These can be sold to help support you in retirement. While you might not decide to sell them immediately, you may want to 10 or 15 years into retirement and this could make a big difference to your financial situation.

If you own a business, you will need to make some big decisions about it as well. You might have the situation well in hand, but if you don't, get some advice from an expert to help you maximise its value. This could mean taking steps to restructure it and boost its appeal to potential buyers. If that's the case, you can't start planning too early. Most self-employed people look upon their business as their retirement nest egg, which is a problem. Business owners trying to sell their business can become frustrated by not being able to find a ready buyer as soon as they retire and so, out of desperation to stop working, are forced to close the business down. Make sure you start planning early and do everything you can to find good advice to help you avoid this scenario. Don't make the mistake of getting overwhelmed by the task at hand and leaving it too late.

Time is your friend

The reality is your retirement could stretch out to 40 years, and you need to keep this in mind when you're planning for it. I usually advise clients to think of it as two stages:

- the first 10 or so years of retirement, when you are likely to be fit, active and open to taking on new challenges

- the remainder of your retirement years, when you are more likely to stay in one place.

For example, it may be that you plan to keep your beach house as a second home for a while after you retire. While there is the added expense of having a second home, it might be an important place for you to recharge your batteries, making it easy to justify keeping it. In addition, it's a useful asset to keep up your sleeve, so to speak, and that might be part of your retirement strategy. If you should be unlucky and find, for whatever reason, your finances don't hold up as well as you were hoping, you have a second property you can sell at some point down the track to help get you through.

Hopefully, once you have read this book you will be able to make solid decisions about planning your finances in retirement, and you shouldn't have to make sudden, unplanned decisions like selling a holiday home. Importantly, realise that your retirement might last twice as long as your parents', which makes it doubly as important for you to make informed decisions about how much money you are likely to need to live on and how you are going to generate that money.

Work longer, work part time

If, after considering what sort of lifestyle you want in retirement and reviewing your assets, you believe you won't have sufficient funds in your superannuation, there are two options you could consider.

The first is to continue working at your current job for longer before retiring. Of course, if you're stressed and exhausted from performing a demanding or physically difficult job, or you have a particularly stressful role, this won't be the best option. If you are already fed up with your current job, speak to your employer about changing your position to a less challenging one, even if it means accepting a pay cut, or think about working part time. Remaining in the workforce, albeit with less pay, will help you reach your goal of boosting your superannuation savings. The impact on your financial wellbeing of continuing to work in retirement will be significant.

Alternatively, you could think about a complete change of career. While you may think no-one will employ you at your age, this isn't always the case. Many employers value the wisdom and knowledge of older workers. You won't know until you investigate your options. It's also possible you will find work you enjoy that is completely different from your current employment. I've had many clients over the years who were completely at their wits' end working in their professional position, who stepped back and found new work that involved very little responsibility and no stress. For these people, the prospect of working another five to 10 years to boost their savings quickly became a blessing and not the chore it was in their previous role. I will explore this topic more in chapter 6, but it is very easy as you get older to shut yourself off from the many opportunities open to you, and they could be anywhere.

The impact on your financial wellbeing of continuing to work in retirement will be significant.

For instance, my father retired at a time when computers were just starting to appear in people's homes. A trained engineer and inquisitive by nature, he was the first in his suburb to have a computer and quickly mastered the basics. Before long, he was giving informal classes to his neighbours on computer usage. These classes became so popular he started accepting payment for them. There are possibilities everywhere, so keep an open mind.

Make every extra dollar count

If you choose the option of continuing to work in your job a bit longer, you will need to sit down with a caring tax accountant who can advise you of exactly how much money you are permitted to put into superannuation and whether you are able to claim any tax rebates or government incentives. One of my favourites is the federal government's co-contribution scheme for low-income earners.

Under this scheme, if you earn less than $50 000 a year and contribute $1000 of after-tax funds to your superannuation account, the government will match it with $500. That's a 50 per cent guaranteed return, which is good money in anyone's book. You simply need to complete your tax return and the money will automatically be contributed to your super account if your taxable income falls below the means-tested amount. Over 10 years, that adds up to an extra $15 000 plus you will have in super.

There is a host of other strategies you can use to boost your super. Another important one is salary sacrificing — or contributing more of your gross wage — into your super as a means of increasing the amount you have to retire on. In fact, there's not much point continuing to work to boost your super if you don't get serious about finding out how much you can reduce your tax bill simply by putting more money from your gross income into superannuation.

Another clever way of boosting your super later in your career is by embarking on a transition to retirement strategy (you will read about this in chapter 4). While the federal government often tweaks this strategy, and it is not as generous as it was, it is a way to encourage older Australians with low superannuation balances to top up their super before retiring and is definitely worth thinking about.

Of course, it's one thing to put extra funds into super, but there's no point in doing this unless you take control of your super and ensure it is held in a quality super fund. Whether or not you add more than the superannuation guarantee—that is, the amount your employer is legally obliged to pay you—to your retirement savings, you want to be able to control where every single extra dollar is being invested so you can tailor your investments to match your tolerance for risk as well as your need for income. Too often people stay with the same old super fund—typically an industry fund run by their trade union, where at best they have a choice of four or five options. These options are usually 'conservative', 'balanced', 'growth' and 'high growth' or something equivalent. If you want to ensure your savings will last as long as you need them to, these options are not sufficient.

Just as you would shop around for the best mortgage to finance your home, you should shop around for the best superannuation fund to finance your retirement.

This means you will need to shop around for a quality fund where you can take control of your superannuation savings. As with all financial products, superannuation funds are constantly improving their offerings and even industry funds are taking big strides in improving the investment options available to their members, so you might find one that suits your needs. You should consider retail superannuation funds, which may be better suited to your needs in terms of the level of control you have over your savings and the flexibility they offer you. Retail funds are different from industry funds as they are usually run by private operators for profit and so can be more attuned to the needs of their individual members. Just as you would shop around for the best mortgage to finance your home, you should shop around for the best superannuation fund to finance your retirement.

You also need to find a good financial adviser who cares and whom you can trust. This is particularly important if you are trying to build your superannuation savings before retirement. I will write more about this in chapter 5, but this is a very important issue. You may feel you have the situation under control and maybe in the early days of your retirement, you do. However, investment options are constantly changing, and as you progress through retirement you will be less likely to keep up with them than when you were younger. A good financial planner will be able to advise you on how you can best do this and suggest appropriate investments that will help you reach your goal. They will also be able to confirm your thoughts on whether you have sufficient super or not, given your retirement plans, and whether you need to build on it to create the retirement lifestyle you want using other options.

Volunteer

While it may not immediately help you boost your superannuation savings, volunteering is something I believe everyone planning their retirement should consider. This is particularly the case if you are still relatively young or unhappy in your current employment but still wanting to do something in the workforce.

Volunteering is an opportunity to give back to your local community and has the potential to completely change your outlook on life. It can make you feel more positive about yourself and your life generally. That's part of the magic of helping other people without expecting anything in return.

The reason I mention it at this stage of the book is that volunteering is also a great way of trying out new occupations. There are hundreds of things you can volunteer for: from umpiring for your local sporting groups to lending a hand to various community social outreach programs and support services. Volunteering can open up endless possibilities and can even lead to paid employment in completely new areas.

You may have to undertake training to progress in your new position, but that's also a good thing. Too often people get to the end of one career and think it's too late to start a second career. It never is. It's all about finding yourself in a different and happier place in life.

Boost your savings

In many ways, the federal government has made life much easier for financial advisers. Simply put, for most people who own their own home and have savings or 'free' assets that can be invested to provide support in retirement, planning for your financial wellbeing is all about superannuation.

This is a big change from years ago. Superannuation was a much more difficult and complicated beast and it was much harder to access those precious funds. Basically, you had to reach retirement age or die to gain access. That's no longer the case. In fact, the biggest challenge nowadays for financial planners, is how to help clients get as much money as they can into superannuation.

You see, money that is held in superannuation is taxed in a benign way. While you contribute to super throughout your working life, your contributions are taxed at 15 per cent and once those funds are in super, any earnings or capital gains are also taxed at 15 per cent. If you are in the workforce working full time, this is almost certainly going to be below your marginal tax rate.

More importantly, once you retire and set up an account-based pension (I discuss these in chapter 2) or your own private pension from your superannuation fund, the assets within superannuation become tax free, both in terms of the income they generate and any capital gains generated by your savings. It becomes like your own little tax haven to support you through retirement.

It is also important to understand superannuation is not an asset in itself. It is surprising how many people get this wrong as there is a big difference. I hear this all the time. People say, 'I don't trust super because a friend of mine lost hundreds of thousands investing in super during the global financial crisis'. Or they might say one particular super fund

Superannuation is not an asset, but a vehicle in which to hold assets.

is a standout investment because it has been achieving high returns for them in recent years. Both comments show a lack of understanding as to what superannuation is and how it can work for you.

Superannuation is not an asset, but a vehicle in which to hold assets. There are lots of vehicles in which you can hold assets, such as in your own name, in a partnership with someone else or in a company. Each vehicle has its own pros and cons. The biggest difference is usually the way assets are taxed within each vehicle as well as some big legal differences you should be aware of.

If you are concerned you don't have enough to live on through retirement, your first thoughts should be to boost your superannuation rather than consider other strategies for increasing your wealth. The federal government decided long ago it would not be able to support the increasing number of older Australians reaching retirement age and chose superannuation as the preferred vehicle to encourage them to provide for their own retirement. As I mentioned, superannuation is important in retirement because it effectively provides you with a tax haven to hold assets in to support you through retirement. At the time of writing this book you could effectively hold up to $1.6 million and have it treated in this tax-benign way.

Once you've accepted that super is the way to go, the challenge is to squeeze as much money as you can into superannuation. The federal government is very conscious many Australians started contributing to super later in life to boost their superannuation savings. For example, former federal treasurer Peter Costello provided in one year's budget that Australians could contribute up to one million dollars into super (much more than previously). This was to entice as many people as possible to contribute as much as they could. This window of opportunity has been steadily reduced. So much so, that one of the great challenges all financial planners face is how to squeeze extra dollars into superannuation as the government moves to reduce and restrict just how much Australians may save in this very effective tax haven.

The current superannuation contributions caps are detailed in table 1 (overleaf).

Table 1: concessional contributions caps

Income year	Date	Your age at this date	Your concessional contribution cap
2020–21	–	All ages	$25 000
2019–20	–	All ages	$25 000
2018–19	–	All ages	$25 000
2017–18	–	All ages	$25 000
2016–17	30 June 2016	<49	$30 000
2016–17	30 June 2016	49+	$35 000
2015–16	30 June 2015	<49	$30 000
2015–16	30 June 2015	49+	$35 000
2014–15	30 June 2014	<49	$30 000
2014–15	30 June 2014	49+	$35 000
2013–14	30 June 2013	<59	$25 000
2013–14	30 June 2013	59+	$35 000

Excess concessional contributions from 2013–14 onwards are included as taxable income, taxed at the marginal tax rate plus an excess concessional contributions charge.

Currently, Australians can contribute up to $25 000 a year, including compulsory superannuation contributions, and claim a tax deduction for it. You can also contribute a further $100 000 a year and not claim a tax deduction for it. There are also special provisions under the three-year 'bring-forward' rule that allow you to effectively make three years of contributions in one, enabling you to make significant super contributions just before you retire.

There are other ways you can contribute to super that are worth mentioning:

- If you sell a business you created, or built up over your lifetime, you can effectively contribute or roll over these funds into super and so avoid paying capital gains tax on the sale. This is a big plus for all those self-employed people who have traditionally looked upon their business as their form of superannuation savings.

As I have mentioned, the big challenge for people who do run their own business is to make sure you don't leave it too late to sell. It is common for those who run their own business to slowly wind down the business as they move towards retirement. This may or may not be intentional, but it does happen. As a result, when they go to sell the business, it is worth much less than it was 10 years earlier when it was operating at full capacity. Be careful you don't leave it too late to sell, particularly if you are depending on it to finance your retirement.

- The federal government recently stated anyone downsizing from their family home into a smaller home within a year of retirement can contribute up to $300 000 — or $600 000 combined for a couple — from the sale of the family home to superannuation. This can be a big plus for those who are concerned their savings are not sufficient to fully support them in retirement. It is a clever way of potentially adding more than half a million dollars to your super just when you need it the most.

Depending on your personal situation, there may be other ways you can squeeze added funds into superannuation. This is where you need good advice because the penalties for getting it wrong are severe. In addition, these rules seem to be constantly changing. Unless you are working in the industry, it can be difficult to keep up with them, so it's a good idea to be advised by an accountant or a financial planner.

To downsize or not to downsize?

This, of course, brings us to one of the most difficult questions people face when retiring. Some people just know they want to move to a smaller home when they retire. They dream of being able to walk to a local coffee shop or, for some, it's the dream of never mowing the lawn again. They know exactly what they want in retirement and can't wait to get there.

For others, it's not so clear. In my experience, clients can agonise over this one issue for years. They can talk themselves into selling but then know deep in their hearts they will be heartbroken to leave a home where they created so many memories. It can even be a constant source of tension where one partner is certain they want to sell and the other is not. It can be a very difficult time.

In my experience, if a client is thinking of downsizing it is because they know they would rather have the equity that is currently locked up in their home sitting in their superannuation generating much-needed income for them to live on. These clients can agonise over the decision for years and then, suddenly, wake up one day and just know. And before the week is over, the house will be on the market.

It's a big decision. The best advice I can give you is to suggest you explore your options if you were to sell. People are often reluctant to sell because they fear moving away from a suburb in which they have lived for decades, or they dread the thought of being in a smaller home or apartment. Others quickly change their mind about staying in their family home when they realise how nice it could be to live in a brand-new townhouse or apartment.

Others fear being 'out' of the property market. I think this is overrated. Their fear is if they sell one property and don't quickly buy another, property prices will jump, and they will miss out. That is always a risk but, in my opinion, it is only a slight risk. It's rare that property prices move by more than 1 or 2 per cent in a year. Given the enormous cost of buying any property, it's not a major consideration and you shouldn't be unduly swayed by it.

Take your time to think through your options and shop around for the ideal property. So often I find clients rush into buying their next property. There's nothing like being a cash buyer, and by that, I mean someone who has sold their previous home, has no outstanding debts to consider and can easily write a cheque to purchase their new property. This puts you in a very commanding position when buying a new home.

There's also nothing like the freedom of being able to move around for a year or two renting different types of accommodation in various locations.

You might find, and fall in love with, a perfect beachside hideaway you never knew existed. And if you are thinking of moving from a metropolitan location to a coastal or country location for a while, then you have even less reason to rush into the next purchase. It seems to be in people's DNA to want to know exactly what they are doing when they retire. But my advice is, if you can, take time out and think through buying your next home.

Stretch your dollar further

This is something most people get very good at in retirement. It starts with the fact most people don't have a lot of debt and if you have structured your finances appropriately, you shouldn't have any debt at all in retirement. This means, of course, you're not paying interest unnecessarily — or effectively wasting money.

Stretching your dollar further can mean simple things. It can mean ensuring you never pay a late payment fee on your credit card again. It can mean making sure you get your full pension discount on your rates notice and electricity bills each quarter. Many people in retirement never pay full price for anything again. In fact, some make this a goal in retirement and this is an excellent way of making your dollar go further.

Take a step back from your life and think through what's important to you. If you have always dreamed of travelling the world, retirement is the time to do it. You have the ultimate luxury in retirement of being able to choose when you travel. You can avoid peak times and school holidays and easily pick up some incredible bargains just by being flexible. Perhaps you'll sell the big family home with all its expensive upkeep and buy yourself a comfortable, small apartment where you can just close the door and know everything will be as you left it, in perfect working order, when you get back from travelling.

Again, think outside the square. If your passion is watching big sporting events (and let's face it, the cost of attending anything these days can be very high), then think about ways you can watch the same event for little or no money. Perhaps you can volunteer as an umpire or attendant. Not only do you get in for free, but you are also likely to feel more a part of things.

These suggestions may seem small or quaint, but they all add up in retirement. They can help you make the most of life without needing a huge income to do it. That becomes important when you read, in chapter 3, about your investment options and how to make the right choices. By having a clearer idea of how much money you will need in retirement and thinking through clever ways of reducing your costs, you might find you can live on a lot less than you thought. It will also take a lot of pressure off you when it comes to making investment decisions.

If you can successfully retire on a limited budget, you will be in a position to select investments that perhaps generate a lower level of income but have the comfort of much less risk. The other benefit of surviving on a lower income, is you are less likely to be tempted to invest in high-risk investments just to get a few extra dollars. This is typically where retirees go wrong. They shop around hoping they will find some magical means of generating more income only to have it end in tears when they find the investment goes bust and leaves a big hole in their retirement dreams.

Living on a fixed income

Unless your heart is set on travelling the world and staying in five-star accommodation wherever you go, it is almost certain you will need less money in retirement than you did before. This is where planning the sort of retirement you're dreaming of becomes important.

It may be as simple as deciding that, as a couple, you only need one car in retirement rather than two. It might be you throw away all those expensive business suits or finally sell the tools of your trade and with them, that ute that's taking up space in the driveway. One way or another, life becomes a whole lot simpler in retirement.

It might be a good idea to put together a budget. Yes, I know — we all hate that word 'budget', but there have been big advances in budgeting software in recent years, making it much easier and more effective to create a budget. These products effectively take 'live feeds', or information, directly from your bank accounts and credit cards and generate tables or charts to show you exactly where your money is going each month. This might sound a bit daunting, but it will save you hours of tedious keying-in. If you're unsure, ask your accountant. They will be able to explain how these budget products can show you very quickly where all the money goes, from all the bills you pay on that big, expensive house you're still living in, to how many cups of take-away coffee you drink.

If you are worried about how much your retirement will cost, putting together a simple budget is a clever thing to do. It will enable you to see exactly where every dollar is going and with that allow you to identify just how much is related to your current working lifestyle and what will naturally drop away once you retire. It can be an eye-opener.

So, while retirement means you're likely to travel and go out less frequently, it usually also means you are spending more time with your family and finding other interests to take up your time.

No doubt, if you find that by necessity you are living on quite a tight budget through retirement, you will naturally gravitate to the things that don't cost a lot but are still fun to do. You will also find lots of others in your age group doing the same. A whole industry has developed — google 'Over Sixties' for an example — that provides older Australians with entertainment at a discounted price. All you need to do is shop around and start talking to people in retirement who enjoy doing the same things you do. The grey dollar is very sought after by restaurants, hotels and event planners. Bargains abound everywhere. The trick, again, is to stay positive and be open to suggestions of new things to try that don't cost much money.

While retirees often fear not having enough money for the first year or two into retirement, this usually fades with time. They become more comfortable living on a fixed or regular income and begin to relax when they find their pension is credited to their account, month after month, along with the regular income payments from their super. They also find new ways to live within their income. Retirement really is a good news story!

So, remember to ...

- *take time out*. Reflect on the sort of life you want to be living in retirement. It could last more than 30 years so it's well worth pausing and taking the time to think about how you want to spend that time.

- *take stock of your life*. Work out how much your home and super are worth and consider any other assets you own, including any businesses. Then decide what you should sell to help support your retirement.

- *plan your finances for when you're in retirement*. Remember your retirement will have a number of phases. You will be more active in the first 10 or 20 years than in the later years and you should plan around that.

- *think about staying in the workforce longer*. Continue to do what you are currently doing, perhaps on a part-time basis, or changing to something completely different.

- *volunteer*. This can be an excellent way of meeting people and it can open the door to a range of new activities that you've always wanted to know more about but never had the time for.

- *make sure you make every cent count*. Contribute as much money to super as you possibly can and make sure you get good advice. Take advantage of any government schemes that might help boost your savings.

- *find ways to stretch your dollar further*. Maybe you need to focus on paying off your credit card on time every time or taking advantage of age-related discounts.

- *vary your expenditure*. Your investment returns will vary with the ups and downs of investment years. Life on a fixed income is very different from living off a weekly wage.

Take a moment to ...

... jot down a retirement plan.

Use this space to write down what you see as the five most important aspects of your retirement. Do you want financial security, for example, or is it more important to you to travel and enjoy your life to the full while you can? There are no right or wrong answers, just what you are hoping to achieve. Be as specific as you can and make sure you include how you're going to fund your dreams.

1. _____

2. _____

3. _____

4. _____

5. _____

Chapter 2
Plan for a truly great retirement

'Just how much savings do I need to retire?' This is the most common question, and the most difficult question to answer, for anyone planning retirement. It's the most common because everyone fears they won't have enough money to live on through retirement, and it's the most difficult because no two people have the same expectations of how they want to live in retirement.

Much depends on where you are in life. If you're in your mid-fifties and happily working in a well-paid job, you might be looking forward optimistically to a well-financed retirement. You might already have considerable savings in super and be confident of building your super balance to above one million dollars, which should easily generate about $70 000 a year after tax to live on. If you are a couple, and you each have about one million dollars in super, better still. You can confidently expect a combined income after tax of more than $140 000 a year in retirement. That's a great situation to be in.

The challenge for you is simply to fine-tune your super. You should be exploring ways to reduce your existing tax bill and further build on your super across the next decade or so while you continue working. In this situation, the answer to how much you need in retirement is 'as much money as you can squeeze into super while you are happy remaining in the workforce'. Once you get to one million dollars in super, particularly if you are part of a couple and your partner has a similar balance in super, you should feel confident and relaxed that you are financially prepared to enjoy your retirement. Happily, this is a situation more and more Australians are finding themselves in.

If you're in your sixties, though, and working in a job you dislike or one that's physically exhausting and you don't have much money in super, the answer may be very different. In this situation, it's a matter of getting to Age Pension age, which varies depending on when you were born (see table 2), and making the most of what money you have.

Table 2: pension age requirements

Period within which a person was born	Pension age	Date pension age changes
From 1 July 1952 to 31 December 1953	65 years and 6 months	1 July 2017
From 1 January 1954 to 30 June 1955	66 years	1 July 2019
From 1 July 1955 to 31 December 1956	66 years and 6 months	1 July 2021
From 1 January 1957 onwards	67 years	1 July 2023

In this case, you need to focus on the day-to-day issues of retirement, and adjusting to getting by on the Age Pension, which might mean making some tough decisions. The challenge for you is squeezing whatever money you can into super with a minimum target of $100 000 before you retire. If you can achieve this, you can expect to generate a regular income of about $500 a month in addition to your Age Pension entitlements throughout your retirement. While this may not sound like a lot, it will make a big difference. Rather than just getting by from one pension pay day to the next, you will have a bit of spare cash. It's a chance to treat yourself on your birthday, for example, or to buy a grandchild a special present.

As more and more Australians benefit from compulsory super, the goal of having at least $100 000 in super is not as far out of reach as it may seem. It should, though, be a wake-up call to those who are self-employed or have been out of the workforce for prolonged periods of time; or who, as the result of divorce, have given up their super to obtain other assets from the marriage. Now is the time to start thinking about getting money into super, even if it's a small amount or if it means working a bit longer before you do retire.

Kill your debts

You need to get your affairs in order by taking some simple steps. The most important of these is to rid yourself of debt. That might sound obvious, but it is surprising the number of people who hope they can somehow continue to live, for example, in a house with a mortgage attached to it and retire. Sadly, it's just not doable. Debt in retirement is the equivalent of financial cancer. It will slowly undermine your financial position and whatever chance you have of providing for yourself.

If you do expect to have a mortgage when you retire, you should think hard about selling your home and finding somewhere you can live debt free. This is not as drastic as it appears, and you should look on it as being part of your new retirement adventure. There are plenty of towns in Australia where housing is very affordable, particularly compared to real estate prices in Australia's major metropolitan cities.

Debt in retirement is the equivalent of financial cancer.

Ridding yourself of debt also applies to any credit card debt you might have lurking around, as well as personal loans and car financing. These are debts you need to get rid of in the lead-up to retirement. Importantly, you should be proactively thinking ahead about setting yourself up in retirement. By this I mean ensuring you have a reliable car to see you through the first couple of decades of your retirement. It doesn't have to be new, but it does need to be reliable and appropriate.

You might choose to spend the first years of retirement travelling around Australia camping. If this is your dream, then you need to start thinking about what car and camping equipment you will need to live this dream. After that stage of your life, you might trade down to something that better suits a more sedentary lifestyle. Either way, you need to be thinking about having a car you can own debt free.

The same goes for where you are living. Think about updating the bathroom, the kitchen and any appliances that are showing a bit of age. It will be more difficult to afford renovations in retirement, as these would place an unnecessary strain on what might be tightly stretched resources if you haven't planned ahead.

Needless to say, if you can't afford these things before you retire, you certainly won't be able to afford them in retirement. If the reality is that your bathrooms and other wet areas desperately need doing up, then perhaps you need to stand back from where you're living now and find somewhere to live debt free that doesn't require any renovations or maintenance. These properties do exist — you just might have to think outside the square to find one that suits your needs.

Not taking these simple steps to prepare for retirement may sow the seeds of disaster for what could otherwise be the best years of your life. The choice is yours. The more you plan and the more steps you take to set yourself up to stop working, the more likely you are to have a happy, well-financed retirement.

Think ahead

The key, of course, is to think ahead. There are few things in life that aren't improved through planning — and retirement is certainly not one of them. The more you think about how you would like to live and the things you would like to do in life, the better off you will be. And while it is never too late to start planning for your retirement, it is never too early to think about what you want your retirement to look like.

Maybe life is good at the moment, and you don't want to make many changes in retirement. That's great. It means you need to focus on paying off any lingering debts and then maximising your savings, particularly those within superannuation, so you can generate as much income as possible in future years. In thinking ahead to retirement, your situation might seem quite straightforward. It still pays, though, to think through a few possibilities: for example, will you still feel the same if your partner is no longer with you or if you are not quite as mobile as you are today? You can't plan for every eventuality, but it is worth thinking about some of the more obvious curve balls that might come your way.

If you are thinking of making a major sea change or tree change in retirement, consider using your long service leave or annual leave to do a few dry runs by spending time wherever it is you're planning to move to.

Two things will become obvious very quickly. Firstly, what felt great during a weekend away might not feel so good if you're living far away from friends and family. Of course, spending time in a new location may just confirm you are making the right choice and that it is the perfect place for your retirement. That would be a good outcome.

> *You can't plan for every eventuality, but it is worth thinking about some of the more obvious curve balls that might come your way.*

Secondly, your new dream lifestyle may be more expensive than you first thought. It may be that house prices are higher than you expected, or you still need a second car to make trips to see friends and family. Unless you can come up with clever ways of financing your retirement dream, that sea change won't become a reality. Much better to find this out before you burn your bridges and find yourself living a life you can't afford or don't really want.

Not thinking through what they want to do in retirement is the single biggest cause of retirees' plans coming unstuck. More importantly, making poor lifestyle choices can put an irreparably big hole in your finances. What might have been more than enough in savings at the start of your retirement can be quickly dissipated through a series of missteps or decisions that appeared good at first but failed to live up to expectations.

Be honest about your needs

Australia is blessed with a very good social security system. It provides an excellent safety net for everyone and includes an Age Pension benefit for those who move into their older years with inadequate savings. Sadly, I have met some clients who shared my father's attitude to the Age Pension. He looked upon Australia's taxation/social security system as a giant bank account. He believed having paid taxes all his working life meant he was entitled to get some of those taxes back in his later years by way of the Age Pension. For good or for bad he went out of his way to set up his finances to ensure he maximised his social security entitlements.

He has long since passed on and with him have gone most of the loopholes he took advantage of. I believe every Australian should try to provide for themselves in retirement. This is not always possible and for those who, for whatever reason, find themselves at the end of their working life without sufficient funds, thankfully there is an Age Pension to help support them in their later years. It's up to all of us to see it for what it is: a safety net to help those in need and not something to take for granted or to abuse.

On the other hand, some people are so stubbornly independent they are loath to even apply for a Seniors Card or a Health Care Card, even though they are entitled to them, much less the pension. If this is you, I think you are being needlessly hard on yourself. You also risk using up your own funds early in retirement and then being forced to rely on the pension in later years. A much better option is to make the most of your Age Pension entitlements if possible and use your own funds to top it up.

Others go out of their way to get the Age Pension even where common sense should tell them they have too much money to be eligible. I remember a potential client arranged to meet with me, having just won a sizeable amount in the lottery. More than half a million dollars. This winning came at the end of a successful and happy life, so it was very much an unexpected and largely unneeded windfall. His sole purpose in speaking to me was to come up with some clever strategy to hide these funds from social security so he could retain his pension. Needless to say, we had a very short conversation.

Likewise, some people try to qualify for the Age Pension and its benefits and discounts by, for example, gifting large amounts of their savings to their children. Don't be one of those people. Although industry figures suggest that, fully costed, pensioner benefits such as discounts on rates and electricity can add up to $2500 per year, ask yourself if this justifies you trying to do anything and everything just to be eligible for the Age Pension.

The only place to legally hide assets in retirement is to leave them in your family home because this isn't seen as an asset when applying for the Age Pension (I'll go into the Age Pension assets and income tests shortly). It is possible to effectively live in a multimillion-dollar home and qualify for the Age Pension, but I don't recommend it. Eventually you will find yourself in a situation where you are asset rich and cash poor and while you may enjoy living in palatial luxury, it will soon come undone when you struggle to maintain the property. If you can provide for yourself, you should.

Your half-a-million-dollar nest egg

Having said that, let's now take a look at the benefits of being eligible for the Age Pension because, if you qualify for it, it is effectively your unseen, unsaved half-a-million-dollar nest egg.

If you're a single person and your assets fall below the assets test limit, and you have little or no income and therefore pass the income test as well, you will qualify for the full pension. The maximum amount you'll receive (at the time of writing) is $944.30 a fortnight or about $24 550 a year. To generate this income from savings you would need to invest $500 000 a year and obtain a steady return year in year out of 4.9 per cent.

So if you think it's too late and you have no money set aside for retirement, think again. You do effectively have half a million dollars just sitting there waiting for you that will generate a safe and secure income stream for you throughout your retirement.

Which raises two key questions I think everyone facing retirement should ask themselves:

- How can I find somewhere to live where I don't have a mortgage?

- How much money can I pay into super so I have a second income stream in addition to my Age Pension entitlements?

If you look at it like this, you will start seeing your retirement in a different light. It will free you up to think more about the possibilities and less about the limitations of your current position. For example, living in a home where you still have a mortgage is a big mistake in retirement and it will trap you into limiting your choices. You should choose somewhere else to live where you won't have a big debt and you'll see life differently. At the same time, scraping $100 000 into super will make a big difference in retirement, generating about $500 a month and freeing you from living from one pension payment to the next.

The Age Pension should be the cornerstone of your retirement plan if your savings are insufficient. Importantly, if you think you will qualify for the Age Pension, you should start applying for it early. As we saw earlier (see table 2), in line with the federal government's goal to slowly lift the pension age from 65 to 67 years, exactly when you should apply for the Age Pension will vary according to your date of birth, but applying a year before you think you will qualify is a good idea. This will give you plenty of time to contact Centrelink and complete all the required paperwork. Be completely honest with Centrelink and they will help you make the most of your entitlements.

Your Age Pension amount is decided according to two tests:

- an assets test

- an income test.

For the assets test, Centrelink will look at all your assets, apart from your home, and determine a true value for them and then calculate the total. At the time of writing, as a home-owning couple, if your assets amount to less than $401 500 you will qualify for a full pension and if you have less than $876 500 you will qualify for a part pension. So, depending on where the assets in addition to your home lie, the more assets you have, the more your entitlements will reduce on a sliding scale. Once you own more than $876 500 you will not be eligible for the Age Pension.

It's also important to keep your eye on these balances through your retirement. The figures used for the assets test increase every six months. If you are close to any of these numbers you may find in the years ahead you do qualify for the Age Pension — or for more than you had been — especially if your investments are hit by a severe economic downturn and drop in value. Remember, the Age Pension is a safety net that is available at any time in retirement.

Tables 3 and 4 (overleaf) set out the full Age Pension and part Age Pension figures used for the assets test respectively as at July 2020.

Table 3: full-pension figures for the assets test

Your situation	Homeowner	Non-homeowner
Single	$268 000	$482 500
A couple, combined	$401 500	$616 000
A couple, separated due to illness, combined	$401 500	$616 000
A couple, 1 partner eligible, combined	$401 500	$616 000

From 1 July 2020, pensions reduce when your assets are more than the limit for your situation.

Table 4: part pension figures for the assets test

Your situation	Homeowner	Non-homeowner
Single	$583 000	$797 500
A couple, combined	$876 500	$1 091 000
A couple, separated due to illness, combined	$1 031 500	$1 246 000
A couple, 1 partner eligible, combined	$876 500	$1 091 000

From 1 July 2020, part pensions cancel when your assets are more than the limit for your situation. Your limits are higher if you get rent assistance with your pension.

The assets test includes all assets except for the house you live in, namely:

- the savings you have in superannuation

- any investments

- any property you might have in addition to your own home.

Centrelink will value your household furniture, cars and any collectibles you own. They will review any companies you might be involved with and any trusts or partnerships. If you are thinking of selling a business ahead of retiring and still hope to qualify for a part pension be aware Centrelink will want to go through all your business dealings to obtain a true assessment of your financial position.

You will also need to pass an income test. At the time of writing, you can earn $4628 a year as a single person in addition to your full Age Pension before your pension is reduced. Centrelink will take into account any income you are receiving from investments and the value of any pensions you might receive from your superannuation (I talk about account-based pensions in the next section).

Two other factors impact your pension eligibility.

- Firstly, Centrelink will 'deem' certain assets as generating an income according to the 'deeming rate', regardless of whether they do or don't generate money. This is to stop individuals parking funds in non-income-generating assets, such as low-interest-bearing term deposits, for the sole purpose of qualifying for the Age Pension.

  On 1 May 2020, the federal government reduced the deeming rates. The upper rate for savings and investments balances above $51 800 for a single pensioner dropped from 3 per cent to 2.25 per cent and the lower rate for savings and investments below $51 800 fell from 1 per cent to 0.25 per cent.

  It may seem unfair that the government deems you to have earned income on savings even if you haven't, but when you think about it, this stops people from abusing an otherwise generous welfare net.

- Secondly, Centrelink also has strict rules regarding gifting. If you plan to give part of your assets away to your children, you can — but you might find these assets are still included in your assets test. Centrelink allows $10 000 to be gifted a year without it adversely impacting your pension entitlements. Any gifts of more than this amount are included in your assessments for the next five years. This trips up many retirees. Say, for example, you have $450 000 in assets in addition to your own home and you decide to give $50 000 to your daughter in the hope this will bring your assets down for assets test purposes, enabling you to qualify for the full Age Pension. Centrelink will accept $10 000 as a gift in the first year, so your assets will be calculated at $440 000 — that is, even if you have physically given $50 000 away and only have $400 000 in assets, Centrelink will determine you have $440 000 in assets for the purpose of the assets test. In the second year, they will determine you have $430 000 in assets; in the third year $420 000 … and so on until they determine you only have $400 000 in assets. It's easy to get caught out thinking there was an error in the calculations and ask your daughter to return the money. This actually makes the situation worse. As soon as your daughter returns the money, that amount is added to your assets. So, in the above situation, you might have started with $450 000 in assets and gifted $50 000 to your daughter only to find that Centrelink still rates you as having $440 000 in assets — that is, $450 000 less the $10 000 they will allow as a gift. As soon as your daughter physically returns the $50 000, Centrelink will add this to your assets of $440 000 and determine you have $490 000 in assets and will adjust your pension payments accordingly. Unfair? Yes. A clear warning to ask before you act? Yes. So remember, Centrelink is on your side, but they have ways of dealing with people who try to bend the rules to their own advantage. My advice is just be honest and accept that if you don't qualify for the Age Pension it's because you have too much money.

In chapter 7, you'll read that while helping family members financially may be what your heart tells you to do, my advice is to focus on looking after yourself in retirement and not on giving your money away — particularly if you qualify for the Age Pension.

Lump sum or account-based pension?

Once you reach retirement age you can legally withdraw all your super savings. The reason people don't do this is because leaving funds in super makes you eligible for some significant tax benefits. It would be a mistake to draw down all your super as a lump sum because this effectively moves it from a tax benign environment into a less-tax-friendly one. Depending on what you do with these funds, you may significantly increase your tax obligations, so you should get good advice before you draw it down as a lump sum. If you plan your retirement and think it through, there's no reason why you shouldn't withdraw a small amount of super to, say, renovate your kitchen or update your car. And you can essentially draw down funds tax free. The key here is to think it through. Every dollar you have in super is precious and is being used to generate income for you. So while it may seem you suddenly have a large pot of cash to play with, when you think about what it is there for — to support you through retirement — you might think again before accessing a lump sum.

Account-based pensions supported by superannuation savings are attractive because they are tax free, both in terms of any income generated and any capital gains that might be achieved by the assets supporting the pension. An account-based pension is your own private pension generated by your superannuation savings once you retire. These funds are paid from your superannuation account to your bank account tax free and are included in the income test calculations. Because they are treated so benignly, there is a large number of rules around setting up an account-based pension. Among these is that the government requires you to receive a minimum amount by way of an account-based pension and this amount increases as you age.

Account-based pensions should be supported by investments generating income as well as strong capital growth. Just what the right assets are will vary over time as the economic, investment and tax environments change and the income generated by the various assets shifts. (I write more about this in chapter 3.) However, this is where having a good financial adviser helps. Not only can they tell you where you should have your funds invested today in order to best support your account-based pension, they should be looking ahead to five years down the track and advising you on what investments are likely to still be performing well then.

There is a little bit of crystal ball gazing to this and no-one can advise you with 100 per cent certainty what will happen in investment markets five or 10 years out. But there are always emerging trends and advisers spend a lot of time keeping abreast of them. In doing so, they will advise you to constantly re-jig your investments to ensure they are in line with your needs and generating as much income as possible while being able to at least keep pace with inflation by increasing in value over time.

Accessing your super early

For most people, accessing superannuation early is not a good idea, particularly if you only have modest savings. Unfortunately, just as the super industry has grown over the past few decades and turned into a trillion-dollar industry, lots of minor industries have developed that feed off it.

One such industry is professional scammers. These so-called 'professional' advisers mostly work in the property industry, coming up with get-rich schemes to help people theoretically boost their super. They work mostly in the property market because this is an easy sell. 'You can't go wrong investing in property,' they advertise confidently. *Wrong!* You can lose money investing in property, just as you can lose money investing in any asset.

It's only natural to want to get ahead and make the most of your situation. However, your superannuation savings are precious and, for most people, irreplaceable, and you should approach every investment idea with this thought front and centre. Any scheme involving withdrawing large chunks of money from super and relatively high fees should be looked upon with distrust. I've seen property deals where, once the promoter has set up a self-managed super fund for you and charged you for their advice, the fees can total 10 per cent or more of your original investment. It's not always easy to spot these scammers and they certainly know their job in terms of separating people from their money.

Most schemes involve setting up a self-managed super fund (SMSF), or your own bespoke super fund, rather than an off-the-shelf, industry or retail super fund. There are often good reasons for setting up an SMSF, but SMSFs can be misused because it's relatively easy for unscrupulous operators to get their hands on your savings. Think carefully before you get involved in any scheme that involves setting up an SMSF, particularly if it means investing in property (there's more about SMSFs in chapter 4). There are lots of sharks out there.

Generally, you should avoid accessing your super early.

You might have a genuine need to access your super funds early. Financial hardship is one. If you have been on unemployment benefits for six months you can apply to your super fund's trustee to release a small portion of your super — usually no more than $10000 a year — to help you get by. Many people weren't aware of this until it was publicised during the COVID-19 outbreak when countless people became unexpectedly struck down financially. If your back is against the wall and you have to do this to, say, buy a new car so you can travel further in order to work, then you have to do what you have to do. At all other times I would advise you to focus on building your super up rather than finding reasons to withdraw super funds.

Generally, you should avoid accessing your super early. Most people retire with too little super and by drawing down funds before or even during retirement, you make the task of financing your retirement much harder. Yes, it is possible for your investments to grow and make up for the funds you have drawn down, but you'll still be worse off than if you hadn't touched your money.

So just how much do I need to retire comfortably?

Most financial planners love this question. It gives them a chance to pull out all sorts of graphs about life expectancy and rates of return, and invariably the figure they come up with is 'at least one million dollars in superannuation savings'. That's their bare minimum, of course. That's okay if you're in your thirties or forties and have time to focus on your savings and on boosting your super. It's less useful to someone on the cusp of retirement, who has nowhere near that amount in super. Bear in mind that in Australia compulsory super wasn't introduced until 1992 (more on this in chapter 3).

As we saw earlier, as a couple who own their own home you qualify for the full pension if you have assets outside of your own home of up to $401500 as at the time of writing. You are eligible for a slowly reducing part pension if you have assets of between $401500 and $876500 on top of the home you live in. If, as a couple, your assets amount to more than $876500, you no longer pass the assets test. This means the federal government has put in place a safety net that equates to an income of about $37 000 a year for a couple.

In addition, you will receive any income generated by your savings. If you have been well advised and contributed a decent amount towards your super, you can expect to receive a tax-free, account-based pension in addition to the federal government's Age Pension entitlements. Just how much depends on how those funds are invested.

As a rule of thumb, you can expect to generate 6 per cent, or $6000 a year, of income for every $100 000 you have in savings. This works out to be $500 a month: an easy number to remember. If you do manage to save $400 000 in super, you will receive the full pension and about $2000 a month from your own account-based pension.

If, as a couple, you think you are eligible for the full pension of about $18 500 each per year as homeowners, this means you will receive about $37 000 a year plus your account-based pension of $24 000 a year tax free — a total of $61 000 tax free. So suddenly life on the Age Pension doesn't seem so bad, does it?

The trick is to contribute as much money as you can into superannuation and then invest it so you are receiving a solid return, after all the fees and charges, of 6 per cent a year. This is a relatively modest return. Even with the conservative stance I take to investing clients' funds, under normal conditions I still hope to achieve a return of closer to 10 per cent a year.

Maybe you'll need a budget

From these simple numbers, you should have a good idea of how much money you will have to live on in retirement. Whatever the situation — good or not-so-good — you find yourself in, the key is to make sure you live within your means. That's essential if you want your savings to last you through retirement.

Depending on how much you have in super, and your lifestyle choices, you might find there is an income shortfall. If you don't face up to this you could make the situation worse and in doing so almost guarantee you'll run out of money during your retirement. But you don't have to. In addition to the ideas I share with you in this book on how you can boost your income and rein in your expenditure, it's a good idea to prepare a 'retirement budget'.

A raft of work-related expenses fall away in retirement. If you haven't budgeted before, or at least not for a while, you may find this a challenge; but once you start, you just might enjoy the feeling of power that comes with knowing exactly where you'll be in retirement.

The good news is there are online systems that can help you. The benefit of these systems is they are very accurate: they take information directly from your bank account and they can show you exactly what you spend in a week or a month at just the click of a button. If you have never done this type of budgeting before, you will be amazed at what you'll find out about yourself.

The additional benefit of this is that after thinking through your financial situation you might realise that you'll have to keep working a few years longer than you'd planned, or that you do have to sell your home in order to repay the mortgage and find somewhere you can live debt free. Sometimes people just lock themselves in the here and now and believe anything else will be a backward step. That's not necessarily the case and you should be open to new possibilities.

Most importantly, sorting out your finances and ridding yourself of past baggage will make you feel better. It never makes people feel worse. You'll be relieved that you're taking control of your finances and sorting out what you need to do to have the best possible life you can afford in retirement.

Be prepared for bad years

It's important when planning for your retirement and trying to estimate how much you need to live on, to be prepared for some bad years. No matter how you decide to invest your funds, all investments have good and bad periods and you should provide for this in your retirement planning.

So plan on the following:

- When times are good and your investments are making good returns, don't make the mistake of assuming they will always make strong returns. They won't. No matter how you structure your investments or how closely you keep track of them, you need to be mindful that the good years will not continue forever.

- Be realistic. Expect a few bad years along the way. Generally, I would expect in every decade to have five good years, one very good year, three ordinary years and one bad year. Accept this and plan for it. Importantly, when you do have a bad year, don't panic and sell everything just because your investments are suddenly not performing as you had hoped. This can be particularly distressing if you face a bad year within the first few years of retiring. Stay strong. Stay on course.

While this can be unnerving, it should never be unexpected. It's all part of getting used to living off your invested funds. So how do you deal with the inevitable ups and downs of investing?

Think hard about the assets you are investing in and what a bad year for those assets will look like. All investments have their ups and downs and it's important you recognise when your investments are going through a rough patch. If you understand your investments, you won't be taken by surprise if they have a poor year and you won't be panicked into selling.

The key to investing and living off your savings is to be aware there will be good and bad years.

Invariably, when I hear people say they lost money during the global financial crisis (GFC), it's because of this one point. They didn't understand their investments and when they saw their capital value drop in line with everything that was happening in the markets at the time, they panicked and sold. Investors who understood their investments, had made good long-term decisions and didn't panic were rewarded. Their investments steadily came back and most investors who didn't sell were basically back where they were before the GFC by the end of 2010.

The key to investing and living off your savings is to be aware there will be good and bad years. During the good years, don't increase your expenditure on the expectation the good years will continue indefinitely — they won't. At the same time, don't panic when the odd bad year comes along. Simply reduce your spending if you can. As I touch on in chapter 5, you should set your expenditure to match the conservative long-term return on your investments. By regulating your expenditure with the income being generated, you will ensure your savings will outlast your retirement.

Have a back-up plan

As with all things, you need to have a back-up plan. For most people, this is accepting that if everything goes wrong, they may have to adjust to living on the pension. As I've said before, we are so lucky in Australia to have a worthwhile social security system. It's the ultimate back-up plan for us all.

If you are fortunate enough to have accumulated some spare assets, you should be able to change tack so you have a back-up plan if things go wrong. For example, you might keep that beach house, knowing that if you're hit by the unexpected you still have that property in your hip pocket to support you if all goes wrong. You could rent it out for a few years or accept that the time has come to sell it.

Or your back-up plan might be to stay in your family home. You might like living there with all the years of memories it contains. You might even enjoy the regular upkeep it demands, such as mowing the lawns and maintaining the garden. Then, if worse comes to worst, you can sell it to downsize and use the funds to kick-start your retirement again.

The federal government has taken steps to encourage this and allows people who sell their family home to contribute up to $300 000 each or $600 000 for a couple to superannuation in 'downsizer' contributions. This can make a big difference to how much you can generate in income from your superannuation savings.

While it is not always possible to have a solid back-up plan, it is important to think about how you will survive if things don't pan out as you'd hoped. If nothing else, planning for your retirement will help you sleep better at night.

So, remember to ...

- *plan ahead.* Think about how you want to spend your retirement and what is important to you. Be realistic about what you will need in terms of superannuation savings, but also be realistic in terms of what you might spend in retirement.

- *repay all your debts.* Retirement is a time to simplify your life and your finances. From that credit card debt you never seem to be able to get under control to that mortgage you still owe on your home. Repaying all your debts is a crucial step in planning your retirement.

- *think about drafting a budget.* This will be crucial in showing where all your money goes if you think life will be a bit tight in retirement and highlighting areas where you can cut back without losing too much enjoyment in life.

- *appreciate your super.* Be careful about how you invest your superannuation funds and think long and hard before making an early withdrawal, no matter how pressing the circumstances or how good the investment seems to be.

- *be honest with Centrelink.* They are there to help you and they will ensure you can maximise your pension entitlements. There are no loopholes or clever strategies for boosting your pension any more—and there don't have to be. The rules as they stand are reasonable enough.

- *be prepared.* Your retirement will cover several decades. There will be some setbacks along the way and some years will feel better than others. Keep an eye on how much money your investments are generating and make sure you spend less than they are generating. If you do, you'll never run out of money.

Take a moment to ...

... write a budget based on your expected retirement income and expenses.

Use this space to jot down what money you think will come in and go out during retirement. This can be a starting point to show whether you can expect to live comfortably within your means during retirement or whether you need to cut back. If you do need to cut back, speak with your accountant about which online budgeting tool might help you rein in your spending.

_____

_____

_____

_____

_____

_____

Chapter 3
Make good investment choices

Retirement savings are irreplaceable. This is the big difference between making investment decisions during retirement and at any other time in your life. You will never be able to go back, retrace your steps and spend another 40 years in the workforce accumulating money.

That's not to say you should become so conservative, so defensive, in retirement that you take on no risk. You can't. The only way to avoid risk completely is to place all your money in a bank account. If you do, though, you will still be losing money because silently, without you ever being aware of it, inflation (that is, the constant increase in the cost of living) will slowly be nibbling away at the real value of your savings. You need to understand the pros and cons associated with investment choices and make decisions based on what best suits you and the level of risk you are comfortable taking on.

This can mean spreading risk across a range of asset classes, which may be difficult depending on the prevailing investment environment, your options for generating money and how much money you need in retirement. For most retirees in the current environment (that is, at the time of writing) this would mean investing a larger slice than they usually would directly into the Australian share market because this is where good income returns can be generated relatively safely. But you need to take care. Shares are not all the same. Either you need to educate yourself so you can recognise the difference between companies that pay stable, high-yield rates of return and those that don't, or you need to find an adviser to help you.

More importantly, you need to feel comfortable with where your money is invested and if you don't, then you should explore other options.

Super really is super

The biggest mistake people make when planning their retirement is thinking superannuation is an investment. It's not. It's simply a vehicle in which you can hold investments such as property, shares or term deposits — or a mixture of all three. Whether your superannuation performs well or not is ultimately determined by how well those underlying investments perform.

What's unique about superannuation is the way it is taxed and the rules applied to it in terms of when you can put money in, when you can pull money out and just how much money you can move in or out at any given time. So, for example, earnings on investments held within superannuation are taxed at a relatively benign level of 15 per cent and not your marginal tax rate. The trade-off for this is that you can't access these funds until you reach retirement age (though there are exceptions).

Superannuation started as an employment benefit for white-collar workers. Mostly men, working in senior management roles. It slowly spread through a number of professions and as most large companies developed their own super funds, with varying rules and benefits, offering access to a high-quality super fund quickly became one way of getting good employees to stay with your company.

Former federal treasurer Paul Keating became something of a champion of superannuation. Australia had long been the victim of boom-and-bust economic cycles. The economy would start to grow, demand for labour would increase, wages would rise sharply, forcing inflation up, which would cause the central bank to lift interest rates, which would cause employers to cut back on staffing and wages to fall. A classic boom-and-bust environment.

Keating saw he could tame this vicious cycle by introducing workplace agreements whereby workers would receive pay increases, but instead of taking most of the money home to spend, a large chunk of it went into their superannuation accounts.

This quickly ended the boom-and-bust cycle that had so long damned the Australian economy. It also had the twin benefits of encouraging ordinary Australians to save for their retirement while boosting Australia's low level of domestic savings.

One of the biggest criticisms of superannuation is that the rules are always changing. This is true and it is a fair complaint.

However, one thing hasn't changed since compulsory superannuation contributions were introduced in 1992: the federal government wants more and more Australians to provide for their own retirement and superannuation is the government's preferred vehicle for them to do so.

So yes, the rules are constantly changing, mainly in favour of giving people more reasons to put money into superannuation by making it more attractive from a tax perspective and offering more opportunities to do so. If you want to save money on your taxes, increasingly the answer is to put money into super. And this has been the case regardless of which political party is in power. More importantly, superannuation is here to stay.

Super is a safe and very tax-effective vehicle for housing retirement savings and if you want to make the most of your financial situation in retirement, you should focus on boosting your super.

Let's talk investments

So you're working out what to do with your savings in retirement and you've realised that you need to use superannuation to make the most of your personal situation. Well done.

The next challenge is to think about creating some underlying investments. Exactly where are you going to place your funds? The best place to start is with term deposits.

Term deposits

Everyone thinks they know what a term deposit is. Right? Yet some of the biggest financial scams and financial losses we've seen were due to people getting this wrong.

And even now, I still see advertisements spruiking bad investments using clever language that makes unwary investors think they're investing in term deposits when in fact they're investing in high-risk property developments.

A term deposit is where you give your money to a bank. Not a finance company, money broker or credit union. This is the key difference. The investment will usually be for a set period of time — six months or two years or longer — and the bank will agree upfront they will pay you the original amount invested plus an agreed amount of interest on those funds at the end of that period. This is all guaranteed. The drawback, though, is that the rate of interest is usually very low: it typically ranges between 1 and 2 per cent.

Term deposits are attractive because the bank guarantees that no matter how much capital you put in, you will get back that amount plus the agreed amount of interest. So if you want to set aside some funds for, say, a holiday next year and be absolutely confident you will get back the full amount you invested plus interest, you might choose to place those funds in a term deposit.

So, the two key characteristics of a term deposit are that they are only offered by banks and that the interest rate is relatively low (and this is much the same regardless of which bank you invest with). Once either of those characteristics is missing — that is, the investment is not being offered by a bank or the interest rate is much higher than the rate offered by the banks — chances are it's not a term deposit, despite what the advertisers claim.

This might sound obvious, but it's the biggest mistake novice investors make. They want the certainty of a bank deposit — the certainty of getting their money back — but they want to get a better return than that offered by the banks.

They let their greed get the better of them and they choose to believe that somehow, someone has come up with a product that can provide a higher rate of return without incurring greater risk. It just can't be done.

If you see an investment advertised as 'safe as a term deposit' but offering you a much higher rate of return, run for the hills. Most likely, this will turn out to be a scheme for raising money to finance high-risk property developments.

The funds will often be used to provide what is referred to as 'mezzanine finance', which is usually the last 10 per cent needed to get a property development off the ground and the first money lost if the project is not successful (I write more about these scams in chapter 4). Believe me, these guys have a way with words and are very convincing. Don't be fooled.

> **The higher the rate of return, the greater the risk. It's that simple.**

There is no easy solution to investing. The higher the rate of return, the greater the risk. It's that simple.

Annuities

Annuities came to life during the deregulation of the Australian financial markets in the 1980s. They were originally promoted by insurance companies as a way of providing retirees with a guaranteed income stream and they do have some attractive features. They are, however, very much a bet between you and the insurance company as to whether you will live a long life or not. Generally, annuities work by retirees investing, say, $500 000 in an annuity and the insurance company agreeing to pay a certain amount each month either for a 10- or 20-year period, or until you die.

The fact that the income offered was guaranteed regardless of whether the share market or property prices rose or fell made annuities attractive. In addition, they were favourably treated by Centrelink and were not included in the Age Pension's assets test. This was later amended so that 50 per cent of the purchase price was included in the assets test, although eventually this too was scrapped. It then changed once more, and annuities again receive favourable treatment by Centrelink.

They remain an attractive option for some because they provide a guaranteed income stream through retirement. However, three significant factors count against them:

- You are taking a punt with the insurance company as to how long you will live because, typically, whatever is left of the capital you invested when you pass on stays with the insurance company. So, if you live into your hundreds, you have made a good investment because you will have used up all your capital, if not more. However, if you buy an annuity and then die within a couple of years, you have made a poor investment because the insurance company gets to retain the capital you invested. This is one of the reasons why they can offer the product and guarantee the income they do.

  They have clever actuaries in their back office working out your life expectancy and making calculations accordingly. They act like bookies, working out what the odds are that you will live a long and healthy life. Again, there are variations on this and it is now possible to link an annuity effectively to a life insurance policy so if you die, say within the first 10 years, you will get back the full amount invested.

  This fact alone often puts people off buying annuities because it can significantly reduce the amount of money left in their estate to be distributed to their children. However, as I write in chapter 7, you shouldn't let that thought dictate where or how you invest your funds. It's your money and you should invest it in a way that allows you to make the most of your life through retirement. Your children can look after themselves.

- Despite the best efforts of annuities providers to generate the highest income they can, there is no denying they are working in a low-interest-rate/low-return environment. So even with the product being structured as a bet on how long you will live, annuity providers struggle to offer attractive levels of income, particularly when you take into account that there will be nothing left of your funds when you die. They are constantly tweaking these products and now offer some that will increase the income paid if interest rates rise. This could be a big plus, although not too many economists see interest rates rising within the next decade.

- If you invest your money into annuities, those funds are effectively locked in place for ever. You can't change your mind. You can't withdraw any of the capital if you need to. Once you have invested your funds, you have no option but to leave them there. Although again, this aspect of annuities has been tweaked and it is possible to obtain an annuity product where you can access part of the capital during the early years.

So there might be a place for annuities in your retirement plan, particularly if you are extremely risk adverse and are attracted to the idea of receiving a steady income through your retirement. Annuities can be used to top up your pension entitlements, for example, and so ensure that all your basic costs are covered. You might then choose to use your other savings to cover discretionary items such as travel or going out. It is also possible to buy a term annuity, which will pay you a fixed income for a certain amount of time in much the same way as a fixed term deposit might. In addition, annuity providers are constantly improving their products and trying to make them more attractive in a world that is becoming ever more risk averse. The market place is constantly changing and it is worth investigating whether there might be an annuity product that suits your needs.

However, it is important that you understand exactly what you're getting with an annuity product. Write down all the key questions you need to ask, such as how much you will receive, for how long you will receive it and whether it will be indexed to the cost of living. When you are convinced you understand the answers to all your questions and you feel the product is right for you, then and only then, should you invest in annuities.

Property

It seems every Australian I meet is having a love affair with residential property. It must be something in the water that prompts otherwise sensible people to believe property, more than any other investment class, is the one, fail-safe way of making money.

I only have to think back to my days as a partner in a small suburban accounting firm to know that of every three clients who held investment properties, two would end up in tears and only one would be reasonably successful. These properties were mostly held by people hoping to minimise their taxes in the short term by holding a 'negatively geared' property — where the costs exceed the rental income — in the vain hope the property would, after capital gains tax, increase so much in value that it would show a profit overall. I could write a book on all the reasons why negatively gearing residential property is a bad idea (and I most probably will one day).

For the sake of this book, though, I'll look at property held without debt by people entering retirement. I do understand why people love property so much. It's a bricks and mortar thing. When you buy a property, you own something tangible that you can drive past and which will always have an innate value.

But, while property values generally do increase over the long term, this is not necessarily correct for all properties. It can be difficult to track when the price of a property falls, although this is becoming easier with so much data regarding individual properties being made available for free online. Property can also generate a steady income stream. If you attract a good tenant to your property, and they religiously pay the rent on time, this can continue unbroken for years.

Still, there are many factors that limit the attractiveness of holding property as an investment in retirement. The rate of return can be low. Most residential property in Australia generates a rental return of between 2 and 3 per cent of the capital value of the property each year. There will always be exceptions to this — for example, many people have boosted their return on residential property by leasing it out in the bed and breakfast space. Good luck with that! While some properties can generate good returns, it strikes me most are a lot of hard work for not a lot more money in the bank — and few people want to work hard in retirement.

The returns on property are further reduced by related costs such as rates and insurance, as well as management costs. If you are still earning income from other sources, you might use these to offset some of your tax obligations, but when you sit down and crunch the numbers, property rarely stacks up as a good investment. There are few tax breaks associated with residential property apart from the attractive non-cash depreciation charges, which usually run out after eight years. Even with the best tenant in a property, there are always the ongoing issues of managing the property, maintaining it and ensuring the tenants are doing the right thing both by paying their rent and looking after the property.

More importantly, when you do decide to sell, you will have to pay capital gains tax (CGT), although you can certainly work to minimise these charges by holding the property in joint names and selling it after you've stopped working. It's best to speak to a tax agent about ways of minimising these obligations.

The other big drawback with property is that any property investments outside of managed funds operating in this investment class are big, expensive investments.

It is expensive to buy residential property in terms of stamp duty and solicitor's fees and it is expensive to sell property in terms of real estate agent fees. Property is also 'lumpy'. By that I mean you can't sell part of a residential property. You either own all of it or sell all of it. You can't sell part of it if you want to upgrade your car, for example.

Depending on your plans for retirement and how much you have set aside to support yourself, property may not be a good choice for you because of the low income it generates. There are, of course, always exceptions.

The key to making sure you never run out of money is setting up your investments so you maximise your income as safely as possible and you set your standard of living or expenditure beneath this level of income.

As I pointed out in chapter 2, it can be a good strategy, depending on your financial situation to, say, hold a holiday home for the first 10 years or so of retirement and then sell it later when you may be less mobile and/or you want to top up the funds supporting you through retirement.

That said, the number-one biggest mistake I see among clients planning for their retirement is that they keep investment properties for too long and live to regret it. They do this because they think they will appreciate in value and if they need to, they can sell them. Instead, what usually happens is because the property is sitting there not generating much in the way of income, it costs more than the overall portfolio is generating. They tell themselves this is okay because 'next year' they won't spend so much and even if they do, they can always sell the investment property. The fact is they are steadily eroding their total capital, and they eventually sell the property when they have little choice other than to do so. By this time, they have whittled down their retirement savings to a point where, even with the sale of their investment property, they are still not generating the level of income they need to cover what they spend.

The key to making sure you never run out of money is setting up your investments so you maximise your income as safely as possible and you set your standard of living or expenditure beneath this level of income. It's not rocket science.

Australian shares

For many people shares are the devil's plaything and nothing can ever convince them to risk their hard-earned money by investing in the share market.

They watch the evening news and see that at times of uncertainty, when the economy dives or unemployment soars, the value of shares comes crashing down.

Just as there are pitfalls in buying property, there are some important pitfalls to avoid if you are investing in the share market, so you have a choice: either take the time to learn what you are doing and find someone you trust to advise you on how you can invest safely in the share market, or stay out of it.

In truth, even shares are becoming increasingly less appealing as an investment because, as I write this, we have entered a period where dividend payments have a question mark over them, making it difficult to generate a reasonable income even through the share market.

The good news is that there's a group of shares often referred to as 'the retiree's best friend' by media commentators that anyone moving into retirement should take the time to investigate. They can provide a relatively safe option for boosting your overall income in retirement. This isn't to say you should invest every cent you have into these shares. You shouldn't, but you should certainly be aware of them.

So who are these 'best friends'? They are large, well-managed companies listed on the Australian stock exchange — such as the big banks and the big miners — that have a long track record of paying strong, reliable dividends. Moreover, they usually pay high-yielding dividends, typically between 5 and 6 per cent of the capital invested in the shares either as a dividend or as income returned to their shareholders or owners.

What's more, for tax purposes these dividends are treated in a way that effectively supercharges their value in the hands of retirees. These companies pay what are referred to as fully franked dividends, which means tax paid on the dividends by the company is refunded as a cash tax refund into the hands of retirees, regardless of their overall income.

This one fact boosts the value of these dividends by about one-third for retirees. A return of, say, 6 per cent on a Commonwealth Bank share 'magically' becomes a return of about 8 per cent.

However, as I mentioned earlier, if the rate of return increases, so does the risk — and these companies' shares are no different. They are listed companies on the Australian share market and so extra care needs to be taken when investing in them.

There are a couple of provisos when it comes to these retiree's best friends:

- Firstly, the value of these dividends is supercharged largely due to the way they are treated for tax purposes — which is not so much a greater return on investment as taking advantage of some clever tax arrangements. Yes, there's always a risk that these tax treatments could be reversed, but it's unlikely, as we saw during the 2019 federal election when the Labor Party unsuccessfully tried to promote its plan to remove these tax incentives as part of its overall campaign.

- Secondly, these companies are the foundation blocks of the Australian economy. While their share value may go up and down, it would take the most extraordinary event to send these corporate giants to the wall, so there is a lot of comfort to take from that. However, any investment in retirement should be made for the long term and investing in the Australian share market is no different. You should always have a long-term horizon of, say, five years and never, never invest money you will need by a certain date.

By that I mean, say you're setting aside funds to finance a trip overseas and you know in six months you'll need $20 000 to pay for the trip. The best place for these funds is in a term deposit where you know you'll be able to recover them in full exactly when you need them.

Do not put these funds into the share market. London to a brick, if you do, when you go to pull those funds out of the share market, the market will have turned against you and your capital will be significantly less than you invested.

So at the risk of repeating myself, never invest funds in the share market if you might need them by a specific date.

The next key to investing in the share market is to remember to buy when prices are low and sell when they are high. Again, this seems so obvious, but it is a frequent mistake made by rooky investors. The reason for it is simple.

When the economy has slowed and the economic outlook is gloomy, this is exactly when share prices will fall. It's also when investors catch that air of pessimism and think the market will continue falling forever. They then decide it's best to sell now rather than endure further market falls.

This is the worst thing you can do. In fact, you should be buying more shares when prices are low. Conversely, the time to sell is when the market is high. However, this is usually when investors get carried away with the euphoria surrounding the markets and believe the market will never stop rising and they wrongly start buying.

This is important even if you're investing in the so-called retiree's best friends. The value of the share price of these companies bounces around just like all shares. The key is to ignore these short-term fluctuations and concentrate on the income or dividends they are generating for you.

Whenever I'm investing funds in the share market for clients who have never done this before, I take a lot of time to walk them through what will happen if the market falls. I tell them if I invest the funds this afternoon and we wake up tomorrow and find the market has fallen by 20 per cent and slashed the value of their investments, we will bunker down and wait for the storm to pass. I tell them that we discussed the original strategy and were confident in the underlying investments and invested the funds

Never invest funds in the share market if you might need them by a specific date.

accordingly. We made these investments knowing we would hold them for the long term and ride out any downturns in the market. It's a conversation I have had many times and a conversation anyone investing in the share market for the first time should have.

The other key to investing in the share market is to diversify. While you may be seeking out companies paying high-yielding, fully franked dividends, don't concentrate your investments in too small a group of companies — for example, by just investing in the big banks.

You might be able to boost your income by doing that, but you risk being adversely impacted by the share market if all four of the big banks are affected by a change in market sentiment. You should try to spread your investments across at least five different sectors such as finance, mining, retail, telecommunications and medical companies, for example.

Here's another thing to be aware of: it's easy to be distracted by companies operating away from the retiree's best friends. Typically, these are start-ups and they bring with them the promise of strong capital gains and the ability to double your money overnight. There's a lot of merit in deciding to invest in capital growth shares, depending on just how interested you are in investing and how much money you have. However, by putting some of your dollars elsewhere in the market, you're reducing your ability to take full advantage of investing in the strong, high-yielding companies and you're taking on more risk. There is more chance these companies won't perform well, will reduce or stop paying a dividend or may even go broke, leaving you with nothing. At the time of writing, the large, listed Australian companies paying high-yielding, fully franked shares are where most retirees will find the sort of returns they can live off in retirement.

International shares

This, of course, brings us to the temptation of investing in overseas share markets — most commonly the US share markets — either via the NASDAQ or the Dow Jones index.

It's a temptation because this is where some of the truly impressive share-market gains have been achieved over the past few decades with companies such as Microsoft, Apple and Facebook. Many of these companies have grown 100-fold. By that I mean investors who put, say, $1000 into these companies have found their investment has grown 100 times to $100 000 or more.

This makes it tempting to invest in overseas markets and, again, depending on how much money you've set aside for your retirement, you could include international shares in your retirement investment strategy. However, be cautious.

It's hard for Australian-based investors to develop a detailed understanding of these companies and how they operate, much less be tuned into what may or may not impact their share price. There's also the double whammy that you have to convert your Australian dollars into, say, US dollars to make the investment and then when you sell or receive income on these investments you need to convert those funds back into

Australian dollars. All too often any investment gains are lost when the funds are converted from or to Australian dollars. It just adds another layer of complexity to the investment process.

A good option is to use a managed fund, which I write about in the next section, as a vehicle to invest in overseas markets. These have many benefits. Typically, fund managers have people on the ground who can develop a better sense of which companies are performing strongly — and will continue to perform strongly — and which are not. In addition, they have teams of experts dedicated to looking at the currency, managing the fund's exposure to it and ensuring any profits made are not lost by moving money across international borders.

Managed funds

For many retirees, placing their savings in a managed fund can be a good option and certainly a worthwhile part of their investment choices. Simply explained, managed funds are where your savings are pooled together with a large group of other people's savings and professionally managed on your behalf.

There is an endless choice of managed funds, with each one detailing exactly what assets it can and can't invest in. Some funds only invest in Australian equities or international equities and some only in Australian property. Others invest their clients' funds in a mix of various fixed-term deposits and possibly corporate fixed-rate debts.

Some funds invest in a mix of assets. Most target a certain type of investor, be it a conservative investor or a growth investor, and there is a growing list of what are called 'ethical' funds, which invest in a restricted range of investments that are earmarked due to their environmental or altruistic features.

Some managed funds are focused on generating as much income as possible and these can be an appropriate choice for people in retirement. As with all investments, there are pros and cons to them.

The benefits are you can select to invest in one or more managed funds and effectively leave the underlying investment choices in the hands of a professional funds manager or investor. There can be some good arguments for doing this: they are experienced, they know what they are doing and they are focused full time on getting the best returns they can.

The downside is they will charge you a fee and, depending on the fund and the way it is structured, this can be quite significant and end up leaving you with less income than you might otherwise achieve by investing the funds yourself.

It can also be hard to choose a managed fund. Do you choose the fund with a high return, even though it might have only achieved those high returns last year because the managers took a punt and got lucky? Or do you choose a fund with a relatively low return because across the long term, it seems to average a relatively steady return?

You also need to be mindful of how much money you will receive after you've paid all the fees and charges. There's not much point in investing in a fantastic managed fund if, after they have deducted all their fees and charges, your return is less than you could achieve by investing the money yourself directly in, say, BHP shares.

Understanding risk

The biggest issue facing all retirees, and I guess anyone trying to manage their own investments, is to understand the concept of risk. It's a bit like fishing. You only hear fishermen talk about their catch when they have landed a really good fish and if you listen closely, every time they tell the story the fish seems to get bigger.

Investing is much the same. Every time you hear someone talk about what a great investment they made, the returns also seem to increase. Just as no-one can rewrite the laws of gravity, no-one can rewrite the laws of investing. The higher the return, the greater the risk. Retirees need to tread a careful line here.

While the focus is on generating income, you need to do so as safely as possible because as I've said before, your retirement savings are irreplaceable. You can't afford to risk, say, losing 25 per cent of your savings because you will never have the chance to go back and recoup those funds. At the same time, you can't afford to leave your funds sitting in term deposits because, silently and eventually, those funds will buy less and less due to the rising cost of living and the impact of inflation. Across the average retirement span of 30 years that can make a big difference.

There's a trade-off between how much risk you are prepared to accept in return for boosting the level of income you want to achieve. As we've seen, you can take a relatively safe course and invest in the so-called retiree's best friends, and as long as you don't get panicked by the inevitable downturns in the market, this should provide you with a relatively safe strategy. If you don't want to invest in shares because they are too risky, your other choices are to invest in property or fixed-term investments.

And don't search for 'fixed term deposits', or the equivalent, that claim to pay significantly more than a traditional bank term deposit. They simply don't exist. Also don't make the mistake of leaving a large chunk of your retirement savings in an investment property generating a low rate of return, thinking it's okay because it will steadily increase in value.

What you want is to choose a range of investments that will generate enough income for you to live on year after year throughout your retirement while still achieving some capital growth. It's important to make good investment choices.

So, remember to ...

- *take the time to really understand any investment recommendations.* Ask the key questions: Is this investment safe, is there a chance the investment will drop in value and what will you do if it does? Is the income generated guaranteed and if not, what might cause it to fall?

- *question if property is the best investment for you*. Do the numbers. Write down exactly how much will come in after you've paid your agent and how much will go out once you've paid all your bills. Remember, retirement is all about generating as much income as you can as safely as you can.

- *consider annuities*. They might have a role in your investment mix, especially if you are extremely risk averse. These products are constantly changing and improving so while there might not be the perfect annuity product for you today, there might be tomorrow.

- *understand how investing in shares works*. Shares can be a bit scary. Their value seems to rise and fall with little reason. At the time of writing, if you want good returns this is where you will need to invest at least part of your retirement savings.

- *look into managed funds*. If you are uncertain about where to invest your money, managed funds might be a good investment option for you. Make sure you understand exactly what the fees are and what the fund is investing in before you make a decision.

- *take baby steps if you are unsure*. Ideally you should start planning your investment strategy for retirement 10 years out. If you don't feel confident, use this time to make small investments. There's nothing like being in the kitchen to understand how something is cooked.

Take a moment to ...

... write a list of your preferred investment options.

Do some research. Think about which investments you think you will invest in long term. Write them down along with the fees you will be charged to make that investment and your likely returns.

_____

_____

_____

_____

_____

_____

Chapter 4

Give up the (financial) smokes!

'Give up the smokes.' I can almost hear you say you did that 20 years ago. Well done. Now it's time to give up the financial smokes. All those bad financial habits — big and small — that you've adopted over the years. They start so easily. And they're always a good idea at the time: the advertisement was so persuasive, or you were setting up a business at the time and it was the easiest way to do it. Perhaps it began with a good idea your accountant had at the time. Now, as you enter retirement, it's time to give up the bad smokes.

But first, some good financial habits

Before I jump into warning you about negative financial habits, let me start on a positive note.

In retirement, simplicity is gold. Your financial affairs should be as simple and straightforward as possible. Have all your savings in one spot, be that in a superannuation fund or using an online investment platform. They should be somewhere you can see them — preferably online 24/7 — and, more importantly, where you can track how much income your investments are generating.

One bank account where you keep some ready cash is all you need. This is where your income — be it the Age Pension, your account-based pension or another income stream — is deposited. You might even want to keep some 'rainy day' money in this account. Then have one low-cost credit card for all your day-to-day expenses. Regular bills such as electricity should be automatically charged to this credit card so they are never overlooked and annual bills such as your rates can be charged to it too. Then, set up an automatic payment to cover the outstanding monthly credit card balance. Set the amount at just below your usual average monthly total spend so the account is always up to date, even if you go on holidays or have to spend time in hospital. Then each month, pay any additional amount that may be outstanding above your usual repayment amount, so you never leave a running balance on the card and never pay interest needlessly. Easy to manage. Simple to run. These are the hallmarks of good financial planning in retirement.

Now let's take a look at the bad habits you should be giving up.

Self-managed super funds

Self-managed super funds (SMSFs) can be an excellent vehicle in which to house your retirement savings. I could write a book just on this one topic. However, almost all the positives evaporate as you move into retirement.

An SMSF, or DIY super fund, is tailor made for you. It's your own personal super fund and you accept responsibility for its running and making sure it abides by all the laws governing super funds in Australia, of which there are more than a few. Typically, you create a corporate trustee and you agree to be the director of it. The trustee company then agrees to run the super fund and hold assets on your behalf within it.

Sound complex? That's because it is. If you're happy running your own business, you will probably be across most of the issues involved with running an SMSF. Most of the tax work can be delegated to your accountant and there are lots of companies that can undertake the administrative work for you. Financial planners can also help you run your SMSF, but at the end of the day you are responsible for it.

SMSFs have become incredibly popular, with more than 500 new ones being set up every week in Australia. They peaked in popularity in Australia during the 1990s when they often provided a cost-effective option for those with more than $300 000 in superannuation savings. Since then, running your own SMSF has become more expensive and comparable funds have become cheaper, so SMSFs are no longer the cheap option they once were. They are also onerous, requiring you to lodge a tax return each year and undertake a raft of other compliance or tax-related activities.

These days the only good reason to own an SMSF is if you own your own business premises. If you are from a wealthy family, it is also possible to set up an SMSF and use it as a tax-effective way of moving assets from one generation to the next. We are just starting to see some clever strategies for enabling this and we will see more in future years as the balance in some of these large, family-owned, self-managed super funds continues to grow. Beyond these examples, there are no reasons for keeping an SMSF and you can create a much easier and more cost-effective vehicle for housing your retirement savings by choosing a retail fund.

Retail funds allow you to control exactly how much of your savings are invested in term deposits, managed funds or direct shares and drill down to identify the specific investment you want to invest in within each of these asset classes. No, you can't invest in direct property investments unless you have an SMSF. But that is yet another reason for not having an SMSF. Once you move into retirement, you shouldn't be holding investments in direct real estate unless you have millions in retirement savings or you own your own commercial premises because you're not likely to ever get the level of income from property you will need in retirement — and retirement is all about income.

Some readers may say, 'I have a self-managed super fund because I have direct investments in gold or diamonds or in a macadamia nut farm'. That's true: you can't replicate these types of investments in a retail fund. But once you move into retirement you shouldn't have these investments for much the same reason as you shouldn't hold direct property in a super fund. These are highly speculative investments that rarely generate income, as I outline in the next section.

SMSFs also need your day-to-day involvement to keep them going and that can be a pain in retirement. During your first decade as a retiree you might remain interested in running it, just as you might enjoy a hobby, but as you get older, your interest will most likely wane. You will also get fed up with the increasing cost and the growing number of bills such as auditor fees, actuarial fees and administration fees.

In addition, there's the issue of what happens when you're gone. I find where a married couple owns an SMSF, there's one partner, typically the husband, who is interested and across all the issues involved with it and one partner, typically the wife, who doesn't know how it's run and doesn't want to. It's quite unfair to run an SMSF and not think ahead to what happens if you're no longer around. If nothing else, you should have a well-thought-out back-up plan. Not having one is irresponsible and will unfairly mean your partner has to come up with a solution at a time in their life when they are least able to deal with this — when they are overwhelmed by no longer having you in their life.

There are some good reasons for having an SMSF and it can be a great wealth-creation vehicle. In retirement, though, SMSFs are unnecessary and cumbersome structures for holding your superannuation savings. Just like smoking, they're a good thing to give up.

Anything that looks like gold ...

It's human nature to look for shortcuts or the easy way out. Such as investing your money in something inert, like gold, holding it for 12 months and somehow magically doubling your money.

Investing in gold is another situation where novice investors get it wrong. The time to buy gold is when it is in the doldrums. When no-one wants it, when no-one is talking about it and when it is trading cheaply. When it is trading at record highs — as at the time of writing — is not the time to invest in gold. You've missed the boat. You might make some modest gains but typically investors who come in late in the day, when the market is hot, hold the investment too long and find the value eventually falls.

What's more, investments in products such as gold generate no income. So you are tying up precious investment dollars in assets that will not make a return for you before you sell them, when you could be investing these same funds in income-producing assets. There's also the problem of physically buying and storing an investment such as gold. There are lots of scammers about who will tell you otherwise, but it's very difficult to invest directly in gold bullion in Australia.

And it's not just gold you should avoid. There is a whole raft of investments such as diamonds, artworks and vintage wine you should steer clear of. Some years ago, when I was a partner in a suburban accounting firm, clients of ours insisted on establishing a self-managed super fund so they could put money into investment-grade, high-quality diamonds. Apparently, there was about to be a dramatic drop in diamonds being mined around the world and the value of investment-grade diamonds would double if not triple within a few years. So they invested half a million dollars in diamonds. In return they received several very fancy certificates validating the investments and photos of the diamonds that were being kept by the company in safe keeping. Eventually the steady stream of information sent out by the investment company slowed and then stopped. An investigation a year or so later showed they had gone out of business. The diamonds, if they ever existed, were nowhere to be found.

If an investment doesn't generate a steady income stream and if you can't easily sell it on a secondary market such as the share market, it is best to avoid it.

Investments with debt

Let's talk about debt. A raft of investments are based on debt. They might be a good idea for someone in their twenties earning a six-figure salary. In retirement, they are just another type of cigarette.

Any investment leveraged or geared up by borrowing money carries a high level of risk. It must. That's what leveraging does to any investment. While it can increase the potential returns, it will always increase the potential losses. It's a fundamental law of investing. Often, debt-laden investments are dressed up as though they don't have any debt. They are based around an underlying property investment and made to look more secure than they are. It can be hard to see the debt element if the promotors don't want you to. However, any investment that involves debt, in my opinion, is just too risky for your precious retirement funds.

Mortgage-backed investments

Mortgage-backed investments can be made to look almost as secure or safe as bank term deposits. In truth, they are the opposite. They are loans to other people and are high risk as they are completely dependent on the other person repaying those funds.

As I mentioned earlier, these investments are usually based around mezzanine financing for property developers. When a developer embarks on a development, they will have some of their own money in the project. A bank will most likely extend a first mortgage against the development, leaving a gap between the available funds and those needed to complete the project. This 'gap' is the riskiest part of the financing as it doesn't have any claim or security over the project.

The higher the return, the higher the risk. It's a simple law of investing that never changes.

Mortgage-backed investments are a very risky form of property development funding. They are never described as such by the promoters and when you do uncover the true nature of the investment, you will be told how safe it is and how certain it is the developer will make a lot of money on the project. If the development was that good, then the bank would have financed the whole amount and there would be no need for mezzanine financing. The higher the return, the higher the risk. It's a simple law of investing that never changes.

Mortgage-style investment schemes are where a company encourages you to provide funding for a property developer to complete a project or perhaps to a finance company to back a portfolio of car loans or personal loans. There are a growing number of these types of companies on the market, spurred on by their ability to promote their services online, both to potential customers and to potential investors willing to drum up the money to be loaned out. Having said that, these companies can be as simple as the old-fashioned solicitor's funds, where solicitors would connect clients with money to clients wanting to borrow money.

Whatever form they take, they exist around the premise of you lending your hard-earned savings in the hope the person who borrows the monies repays them. In return for investing your money, you will usually receive a regular 'interest' payment, either quarterly or half yearly, and at the end of the project hopefully receive your capital back in full. These investments are entirely dependent on the developer's or financier's success in running the project, not running out of cash and bringing the matter to a successful conclusion.

These schemes can vary in almost every aspect, but mostly they vary significantly in how secure or not secure the investment is. They are always unlisted, so your money can be locked up for a protracted length of time and you might find it difficult to get it back if things start to go wrong.

Invariably, these investments are promoted as being bullet proof — that is, that you are lending money in the form of a mortgage and (often) that it's secured by property. In addition, you are being lured along by the prospect of extra high returns on what is being promoted as a super secure investment. Of course, this alone should set red flags waving in your head. Super secure returns and high returns just don't go together in this world.

The real question you should be asking yourself in this situation is, if this is such a good investment why are the hundreds of banks and commercial lenders, who have been extending this sort of finance for decades and who make their living from assessing these sorts of projects, not taking advantage of this opportunity? The answer is they have looked at the project or concept and decided it is too high risk. And typically these sorts of small developers or financiers shopped their project around to lots of potential backers before it reached you and it has been rejected time and time again because the level of risk as assessed by those working in the industry has been rated too high and they have walked away.

This should be all you need to know to prompt you too to walk away. I believe there are much better, safer investments, as outlined in chapter 3, that will serve retirees, and those close to retirement, well — not just now but for decades to come.

Margin loans

While high-yielding, fully franked, dividend-paying companies are known as the retiree's 'best friends', borrowing money in retirement to ramp up your exposure to these best friends is wrong. It's like hanging out with the cool kids at school who drink and smoke and drive cars illegally. It might be fun at the outset, but it will only get you into trouble.

Margin loans are easily available. They are borrowed funds secured against a bundle of shares you already own as well as the new shares you will be borrowing the funds to buy. For example, you might own $10000 worth of shares and borrow a further $10000 to buy another tranche, giving you $20000 of shares in total against which $10000 in debt is secured.

In doubling your exposure to the market, you will effectively double your dividends and if you buy companies paying high-yielding, fully franked dividends, you will double your franking credits. In a low-interest environment, the income generated on this bundle of shares would be more than the interest you have to pay on the loan. On the face of it, this seems like a clever way to boost your income in retirement.

Margin loans can be attractive to people on high incomes, who use them as a form of 'negative gearing' where instead of using property, they use shares. The interest on the loan and other associated costs can be offset against the income from the shares and any shortfall can be used to minimise tax obligations on other sources of income. Rather than investing in shares that pay high dividends, this strategy usually involves investing in companies whose share value is expected to rise quickly.

Regardless of the strategy, the risk with any margin-lending-based investment is if the market turns and the value of the shares suddenly drop, you risk breaking the debt-to-asset value attached to the loan when it was put in place. Typically, this is set at about 60 per cent. This means the debt can never be worth more than 60 per cent of the value of the shares. That sounds a safe margin until suddenly the market moves against you and it isn't. If the share's value drops below this ratio, you will receive a 'margin call', forcing you to sell shares until the loan's asset ratio falls back into line with the original agreement. The downside is you are forced to sell shares at exactly the time you should be buying — when prices have fallen. It's an easy way to lose a lot of money and can be a tough lesson if you are learning it for the first time in retirement.

If you're retired, it's best to avoid any investment with a margin loan attached to it in any form.

People usually invest using margin loans until the market moves sharply against them and they are forced to sell. In terms of a suitable retirement investment, margin loan products fail on several fronts. They can be difficult to understand and you will need to spend a lot of time keeping an eye on the market to avoid being forced to sell should the market suddenly fall. It's a lot of risk for a small increase in income.

Remember Storm Financial, the Queensland-based financial services business that crashed in 2009 after giving inappropriate financial advice to more than 3000 investors? It's a perfect example of margin lending resulting in an incredible destruction of superannuation savings. Storm's financial advice centred on effectively doubling one margin loan on top of another and borrowing against homes to invest in the share market.

Bottom line: if you're retired, it's best to avoid any investment with a margin loan attached to it in any form.

Risky trading

Risky trading products are where you buy or sell what are called 'contracts for difference'. These are complex financial instruments bought and sold based on the value of another asset, usually shares. In buying these investments, you bet on whether the value of the underlying assets will increase or fall. If you get the bet right, you make money; if you get the bet wrong, you lose money.

The stinger in trading contracts for difference is they allow you to leverage up your investment — and leverage it significantly. A contract for difference allows you to bet on the value of another asset increasing and decreasing, but you only need to put a small amount of the money at stake upfront to acquire the contract — often as little as 1 per cent of the full value of the contract.

This is the main attraction of a contract for difference. Even if you don't have the money to buy the underlying asset itself, you can share in potential gains and losses of its value. As your trading is leveraged, the gains and losses are magnified, and the risks are much greater. So much so you can end up losing more than you put in. A lot more. And like any betting structure, the temptation, once you start losing money, is to chase your losses hoping to win them back. Too often, you end up losing even more money.

A tax accountant I once worked with told me of a client who had retired with more than one million dollars in his self-managed super fund. He then attended a so-called trading seminar and got hooked on trading contracts for difference. I use the word 'hooked' advisedly, but in truth that's what it was. Just as many people get hooked on gambling, he got hooked on trading contracts for difference.

Within two years he had lost almost all his retirement savings and that was after having a year of losses scrutinised by his accountant when he did the annual returns for the fund and being told by his accountant to stop trading. In the end, the client lost so much money he had to return to work.

People get carried along by the sales hype and choose to overlook the obvious risks of these strategies. Then, once they start losing money, they feel under enormous pressure to win back the lost capital; instead of stepping back and thinking this is the wrong investment for them, they just keep losing money.

Capital guaranteed or protected products

Many investment products are promoted as being capital guaranteed, or protected, so they may on the face of it appear perfect for risk-averse retirees. For example, you might be encouraged to invest in a managed fund that is a 'capital protected' investment. It might be linked to Australian shares. It might offer to pay investors a return equal to 80 per cent of the cumulative growth in, say, the S&P/ASX 200 share index over, say, five years. The promise might include a guarantee that if the cumulative growth turns out to be negative, you will still get back the original amount you invested at the end of the five years. That's how so-called capital protected products work, and if that all sounds complex, it is — and that in itself should be a red flag that these investments are not for you in retirement.

No two capital guaranteed or protected products are the same. Most are for a fixed term, generally five years or longer, and fees usually apply if you want to exit before the term is complete. The guarantee or protection generally only applies if you hold your investment for the full term and invariably they come with associated costs that may or may not undermine the value of making the investment in the first place. Investments can be guaranteed in a range of ways either by taking out insurance or some sort of hedge facility.

The biggest enemy of a secure and sustainable financial future in retirement is high fees and charges.

Before you invest in a capital guaranteed product, understand they are often promoted as being the same as a term deposit, but they are not. They are highly complex, heavily engineered financial products where there are lots of moving parts, meaning lots of ways to lose your money. If you want the security of putting your money in the bank knowing you will get your money back in a year or two plus interest, you are better off putting your money in a bank and accepting the lower interest rate.

Complex financial products are always expensive. Someone has put a lot of time and effort into creating them and they will want to be rewarded for their efforts. These products won't be promoted as being expensive. They will be promoted as offering you a secure investment with a higher rate of return and the marketing will emphasise how clever you are to have found them. Remember: the biggest enemy of a secure and sustainable financial future in retirement is high fees and charges. This factor alone means you should avoid capital guaranteed or protected products.

And be warned: a guaranteed product is only as good as the company making the guarantee. If the company promoting or supporting the product goes broke, then the guarantee becomes meaningless. The trap is that often products are promoted as being guaranteed by a large financial institution and in some cases even by a bank. Be careful. Read the fine print. Invariably the guarantee will be offered by a subsidiary or associate of the large financial institution and when things fall apart, you will find there is a lot of distance placed between the company you thought was providing the guarantee and the company actually making the guarantee.

Until you read the product disclosure statement issued with the investment carefully, you won't know who is guaranteeing the money. You might be disappointed to read it's not the company you thought was standing behind the product. As these products are so highly structured it can be extremely difficult to get your money out early should you need to, which is another reason for not investing precious savings in them.

Unlisted investments

A lot of investors get confused by the terms 'listed products' and 'unlisted products' and the real difference this makes to their investments. An investment is listed if you can buy it on an established secondary market. A good example of this is the Australian share market. You can invest your funds in companies listed on the Australian share market by buying and selling them whenever you want. This is important as it means you can get out of an investment at any time. You might have to accept a lower price for the investment than you might have paid elsewhere for it, but you can always get your money out of it by selling it. There are other secondary markets for investments, but the Australian share market is the primary one.

An unlisted investment is one not listed in a secondary market, where you need to deal directly with the company issuing the investment if you want to acquire or sell it. A raft of unlisted investments might be recommended to you in retirement. These include such things as unlisted debentures and unsecured notes, which are both forms of lending to large companies. Managed funds are another example where you have to apply to the manager or company running the fund to acquire or sell units in it. Most of the time these events happen easily and without issue, but you can run into unforeseen difficulties with unlisted products.

For example, during the GFC many retirees had funds invested in mortgage funds and these were by and large considered appropriate retirement investments at the time. These funds pooled monies from a large number of individual investors and then loaned out these funds as mortgages or funds secured against property. They paid a slightly higher rate of return than a term deposit and were considered a relatively low-risk investment.

However, during the global financial crisis, the federal government took the step, which many believed was unwarranted, of guaranteeing bank deposits to supposedly avoid a run on the banks. This merely increased investors' nervousness at the time and while it stopped a run on bank deposits, it prompted many to be concerned about money invested in mortgage funds.

Investors decided to call on their mortgage funds to redeem their investments or sell their units and most funds 'froze'. As mortgage funds invest their clients' money in long-term loans or mortgages, many funds quickly faced a liquidity problem in releasing funds and had to freeze investments. This meant investors couldn't redeem their funds at any price. Eventually these funds slowly 'un-froze' and investors were able to get most of their funds back, but it was a difficult period. It proved a valuable lesson in the value of only investing in listed assets where you know you can always sell your assets, even if it means taking a reduced price.

Super strategies

Wherever you find people with money, you will find other people trying to relieve them of it and spending increasing amounts of time coming up with clever strategies to do just that. Since superannuation was introduced, there has been an increasing number of Australians sitting on large pools of retirement savings who have never before had the experience of managing such large amounts of money. Unfortunately, they often make easy targets for the unscrupulous trying to take advantage of them.

Your superannuation savings are precious and irreplaceable.

Many schemes promoted these days focus on accessing your superannuation savings. Too often they revolve around so-called property deals as this gives them an air of security that it's impossible to go wrong if you're investing in property. As we saw earlier, at the same time, they usually involve establishing an SMSF. Not only does this give the promoters another avenue for charging you large set-up fees, it also makes it easier to access your super. As you are the trustee of the SMSF, you can dictate where the funds are invested. You can easily access the savings by simply writing a cheque. The ease with which funds inside an SMSF can be accessed can quickly become a slippery slide and before long you may find you've spent a lot of money without much to show for it.

Accessing your super early should be a big red flag. Unless you are sitting on several millions worth of retirement savings you should avoid such strategies at any cost. Your superannuation savings are precious and irreplaceable. They are there to provide for you in retirement. It will be almost impossible if you start playing around with your superannuation and reducing the balance by accessing it early.

One of the few strategies worth looking at that involves accessing your super early is the transition to retirement strategy. This was introduced by the federal government to encourage older Australians to stay in the workforce longer either by cutting back on their working hours or by increasing their pre-tax super contributions. The strategy provides for you to contribute extra funds to your super fund from your gross income — and so effectively divert funds that would otherwise go to Canberra in the form of income tax — and send those funds to your superannuation account. A pension is then drawn down from your super fund, giving you early access to your superannuation. This pension, or regular payment, tops up your after-tax income so you are left with the same amount of take-home pay, even though you have reduced the hours you work or increased your super contributions.

It sounds a bit like a merry-go-round and you might wonder why bother. The reason why you would bother is if the strategy is set up correctly by your accountant or adviser, it should lead to you boosting your overall superannuation balance.

The only times you should attempt to access super early are for a transition to retirement strategy or if you are facing extreme financial hardship. If you can't make an investment within the confines of your superannuation fund or without setting up an SMSF, you shouldn't be making it at all. The rules governing super-based investments are there to protect your super savings. Any investment strategies that involve you setting up an SMSF and writing a cheque to a so-called promoter who draws on your retirement savings should be avoided at all costs.

Too-good-to-be-true investments

Going back to my days as a finance journalist, it amazed me how easily people parted with their hard-earned cash and got swept along by investments that by any measure were just too good to be true. And despite all the education over the years and efforts by the Australian Securities and Investments Commission (ASIC) and the federal government to alert investors to the more obvious scams out there, investors just never seem to learn.

ASIC reports shonky investments and scammers are more prevalent than ever and sadly even people who should know better — those who are in their fifties or older — seem to be the most vulnerable to being scammed or taken advantage of. (I write more about this in chapter 8.)

Of course, this is where I have to say if an investment sounds too good to be true, it probably is and you should walk away. That sounds obvious and most would think that's all I need to write on this matter, but sadly the statistics from ASIC show this remains a big problem.

Many people are spurred on by the media and the heavy focus in today's society on those who have achieved great wealth in their lives — and by that I'm referring to people such as Bill Gates and Steve Jobs, who went from being ordinary people to billionaires seemingly overnight. Over the centuries there have always been business people who found themselves on the wave of new technology or social changes and who, combined with a huge amount of hard work, cleverness and a degree of luck, have been able to transform that situation into incredible wealth.

This, though, is different from finding yourself in a conference room or hotel setting and being lectured by so-called investment advisers about how you can take control of your life and double your money overnight. Take your time and be extremely cautious. Read through the information in detail and if you see big commission fees and estimates of over-the-top returns, walk away.

We can all learn more about investing and if you are interested in learning more, that's a good thing. There are caring, legitimate financial planners out there who put on information nights as a way of meeting new clients and who do so by providing them with free, legitimate advice about their retirement planning.

Don't invest in anything you don't understand

Not investing your precious superannuation savings in anything you don't understand also sounds a bit obvious, I know. However, you would be surprised at how many people who have lost significant amounts of money have said to me, 'well I didn't really understand it, but I trusted the adviser'.

No-one expects you to be an expert on investing. Most people find the topic of investing funds very boring and it is only the terrifying thought of how they are going to survive financially in retirement that prompts people to think about their superannuation at all. However, there is a big difference between becoming an expert and going along with an investment you don't understand because a very articulate sales person is convincing you that you should invest in some fancy scheme.

What these sales people are preying on is that you will feel too embarrassed to own up to the fact you don't understand what they are talking about and you will go along with them and agree to invest your money. You are not alone. Nobody likes to feel foolish or that they don't understand something the other person portrays as simple and straightforward. It is much easier and less embarrassing to just nod your head and sign on the dotted line than to repeatedly ask questions.

The bottom line here is that it's part of the job of the person advising you to make sure you do have a reasonable understanding of the investments they are putting before you. You don't have to be an expert on the investment but you do have to develop a reasonable understanding of where your money is going, what it is being invested in and, most importantly, how it is going to be returned to you and when.

While a lot of people feel uncomfortable asking questions, fearing this will show how little they know about an investment, the opposite is true. Astute investors always ask questions and are fearless in persisting until they have satisfied themselves they understand what is going on, what all the fees and charges are and what the pros and cons of any particular investment are. In fact, asking lots of questions is usually the hallmark of an interested and well-informed investor.

More importantly, your adviser should never be exasperated by you asking questions, nor should you ever feel you are wasting their time by asking them. It's only by asking questions that you will understand what is happening with your money and that's in everyone's interest. Your adviser should be able to simplify whatever investment strategy they are putting before you to a point where you do understand and they should never tire of explaining it to you.

Investing money is complex and you have a right to be concerned. You also have every right to continue asking questions until you are satisfied you understand what is involved in a particular investment strategy. Just pause and think about how you would feel if you lost all the money you invested. If nothing else, that one thought should prompt you to keep asking questions until you are fully informed.

So, remember to ...

- *only keep an SMSF in retirement if you have a specific reason for it.* They can be great wealth-creation vehicles, but not in retirement. For most retirees there are better, cheaper and less time consuming superannuation vehicles you can use while still having control over your investments.

- *avoid any investment with debt.* Debt may increase the potential return but it will certainly increase the level of risk. In retirement, any debt is carcinogenic and best avoided.

- *steer clear of complex products that you can't understand.* Contracts for difference are just too high risk, and capital-guaranteed products are typically too expensive when you work through the numbers. Just like raw fruit and vegetables, simple investments are best in retirement.

- *beware of scammers.* They are everywhere and many are focused on getting their hands on your super. Avoid any investment strategy that involves accessing your super early and/or involves complex property arrangements.

- *steer clear of anything you don't understand.* If you can't explain back to a financial planner what they are proposing you should invest your retirement savings in, then don't do it. It's that simple.

Take a moment to ...

... take stock of any financial smokes you've considered investing in.

Toss them away and write a list of good financial habits you'd like to adopt in retirement.

_____

_____

_____

_____

_____

Chapter 5
Live like a millionaire

Live like a millionaire! It's the stuff of our generation. Everyone wants to have a million dollars. Everyone wants to be a millionaire. Everyone wants to live like a millionaire. But what does it mean?

For most, it's not about dollars in the bank. That's part of it, but not all of it. It's living with financial security. It's knowing your bills will be paid when they fall due and that you will never be caught short of funds. It means living a comfortable lifestyle. Enjoying the occasional treat, and perhaps that special trip overseas. Enjoying your life.

Just how you perceive yourself will largely depend on your own mindset. I have clients who live quite happily in classic old fibro cement shacks by the beach and others who appear to be extremely unhappy in themselves even though they live not so far away in beautiful homes and have significant savings in super — and more.

Ultimately, what will decide whether you are happy or not in retirement — whether you believe you are living like a millionaire — will be your perception of your situation. Decide what you believe is important in your life and make decisions that support those choices. You will no longer be working, so that's one box you've ticked. Sort out your finances so you can live within your means whatever your level of income. Sort out any financial issues you might have at the start of your retirement. Make the most of every day as it comes along. Ultimately, it is how successful you are at these challenges, rather than how much money you have in the bank, that will determine whether you're happy in retirement.

It's all about income

Managing your finances in retirement is the key to a happy retirement. Retirement is all about generating as much income as possible as safely as you can while trying to keep pace with inflation in terms of the value of your investments.

It's a time for making conservative, thoughtful decisions. The funds you invest are literally irreplaceable. They are precious. When you are making investment decisions, these thoughts should be front and centre.

That's when you'll be living like a millionaire—when you're happily living off the income generated by your investments.

This is not a time for proving you know more about the investment markets than your accountant or financial adviser. It's not a time for being carried away by promises of get-rich-quick schemes. It's not about finally getting your hands on a chunk of money and proving you can play the share market.

It's about taking well-thought-out, considered steps focused on how you can generate as much income as possible while minimising the risks.

This means many investment products are not suitable for you at this stage in your life. And it's not necessarily that these investment products are bad. They're just not appropriate. You need to seek out investments you understand that generate high levels of income, are simple and straightforward, and will still be around in the future. Then you need to structure your life so you are living within the limits set by the level of income you are generating. That's when you'll be living like a millionaire — when you're happily living off the income generated by your investments.

Financial advisers: do I need one?

The recent Hayne Royal Commission into Misconduct in the Banking, Superannuation and Financial Services Industry made it appear like almost every financial planner in the country was a crook.

It did uncover a lot of wrong-doing in the industry and implemented some much-needed changes that were long overdue. Outlawing the ability to charge fees for no service and charging undisclosed commission fees to client accounts were among the most important changes.

But these changes only impacted a small percentage of the industry. Most financial planners had already started to move beyond these fee structures, and it is now considered best practice for a financial adviser to charge a flat fee, much the same as an accountant or solicitor does when providing you with advice.

The issues surrounding superannuation and retirement these days are so complex, most people have little choice but to seek out a financial planner and more importantly listen to their advice to make the most of their financial situation as they move into retirement.

A lot depends on the individual. It's a bit like having your tax return completed for you by a tax agent. It is becoming increasingly easier, particularly for pay-as-you-go wage earners, to go online to the Australian Tax Office portal and complete their own tax return. This is very much the case if your income is relatively unchanged from last year and your expenses are much the same. If you are in this position, why not complete your own tax return online where most of the information is pre-populated for you anyway?

However, if your immediate response is 'no, I don't want to do that, I don't feel confident enough', then you shouldn't. You should take advantage of the fact the money you pay a tax agent to complete your tax return is fully tax deductible and have it completed professionally on your behalf. If nothing else it will give you the confidence that not only has it been done, it has been done correctly.

Your financial affairs are more complex than completing your tax return online, particularly as you move into retirement. Getting your finances structured correctly can be a challenging task. If you don't feel confident about making financial decisions, you should definitely find a good financial planner to guide you. There is a lot of ground to be covered. If you think you will qualify for the Age Pension, then you should take the time to make an appointment and meet with a Centrelink employee to work out your entitlements. It can be difficult and time consuming dealing with a bureaucracy such as Centrelink, and there few less pleasant things to do in modern Australia than sitting in a Centrelink office waiting to meet with one of their officers.

... successful millionaires surround themselves with good advisers.

However, it's just something you have to endure. Take a deep breath and a good book to help you get through it. Most Centrelink employees are hard-working, committed individuals who want to see you get every cent you're entitled to. They are there, though, to make sure you don't get more than you are entitled to, and that's fair enough too.

If your affairs are complex and you have significant superannuation savings or you own businesses or a number of properties, then you definitely need to meet with a financial planner. The rules governing superannuation are just too complex for you not to be guided by a well-trained, highly qualified professional.

One of the foundation stones of living like a millionaire is that successful millionaires surround themselves with good advisers. There is a reason for that. It pays to be well informed, particularly when it relates to getting the best advice you can regarding your money. This is not an area to cut corners. Your retirement savings are just too precious for you not to get good advice about.

How do I choose a financial adviser?

The answer to this question comes down to whether or not you want to be involved in sorting out your finances. That might sound strange, but in my experience, financial planning clients can be broken down into two groups:

- those who are diligent and happy to spend time shopping around, speaking to a number of financial planners and comparing the pros and cons of signing up with one.

- those who just want their finances sorted. They don't really want to talk about it. They don't want to dive in deep because they are afraid they will be embarrassed by their lack of understanding of financial products or embarrassed they haven't saved more for their retirement.

  These clients just want to close their eyes, hand their information across to an expert and cross their fingers the financial planner does an honest and effective job for them.

  No matter how much the federal government or its overseeing body, the Australian Securities and Investment Commission, want to believe clients like this don't exist, the reality is they do. And even though you have taken the time to purchase and read this book, there is a good chance this is you.

If you plan to be diligent in your choice of financial planner, shop around, meet with a number of financial planners and take notes. The first meeting should be free of charge and it should be an opportunity to meet each other and for you to decide whether there is chemistry between you.

I'm assuming every planner you meet with is duly licensed and qualified. If they are not, or if they say they are still getting their qualifications up to scratch, walk away. While significant changes have been made to the industry recently, every financial planner in the country has had enough time to get up to speed with them. There is no excuse for anyone who portrays themselves as a financial planner to not be up to date with their qualifications. Once you have determined this, you should meet with three or four other financial planners and decide who is the right fit for you.

Your choice of financial adviser might be all about how you see yourself in retirement and how much you think you can generate in terms of income based on your savings. It will involve feeling you can trust them and that they genuinely have your best interests at heart. When you've found that 'right' person, you need to be brave. If you have any concerns, perhaps start off with baby steps and invest a portion of your retirement savings with them to see how that goes. If you are happy with them, you can slowly start investing more money through them and gradually move to a place where you entrust them with your entire life savings.

Here are some characteristics you should look for in a financial planner. If they don't tick these boxes, you should walk away.

- *They should be approachable.* You should feel you have a rapport with them. That even when things get tricky, they will take your phone call or at least get back to you promptly.

- *They should charge a set fee.* This will always seem high, but you get what you pay for in this world. Financial planners carry a lot of overheads and a lot of invisible costs in terms of training and keeping their knowledge up to date, so unless they are charging you a reasonable rate, they will quickly go out of business. Make sure they charge a set fee regardless of how much money you have invested with them and that they don't receive fees or commissions from any other party. This will ensure the advice they provide is and will always be in your best interest.

- *They should simplify things for you without you feeling they are speaking down to you.* They should be able to unravel the most complex financial issues to a point where you understand what is happening. That is a big part of their job.

I know shopping around and talking to financial planners about your finances and forthcoming retirement is about as exciting as having dental work done, but trust me: if the financial planner can't tick these three boxes, then you need to keep looking.

A changing dynamic

While it's obvious to say people planning for their retirement need to seek out high-income-generating investments offering a reasonably low level of risk as well as some capital growth, the challenge is achieving this balance.

What's right for you will vary depending on your personal situation and the state of the economy and investment markets generally. At the time of writing, the bigger, well-established companies listed on the Australian share market — which I have previously referred to as the retiree's 'best friend'— should be part of the mix (see chapter 3).

Investing directly in the Australian share market can be challenging for first-time investors. If you are concerned about risk and getting your money back when you need it, you could keep a pool of funds — perhaps one or two years of income — invested in term deposits or as cash in a bank account. You might put in place a series of rolling term deposits, where each one falls due for renewal on a different date — for example, they might stretch from three months, to six months, to 12 months. That way, you'll regularly have access to an amount of cash and so will never face the need to sell precious investments in the share market cheaply should you need money at a time when the share market, and so your investments, are at a low point.

Never invest all your funds in one asset (including the share market).

Reducing the amount of money you have invested in the share market by moving some funds into cash or term deposits has two benefits:

- It can significantly reduce the risk of investing in the share market.

- It avoids the potential challenges of accessing cash at short notice.

What do I mean? Never invest all your funds in one asset (including the share market), particularly if you are relying on those funds for a regular source of income. You should diversify.

Consider having a mix of cash, term deposits, annuities and managed funds. Exactly what the right mix is will depend on you.

You should retain at least a year's worth of income in cash in a bank account. Some advisers will increase this to two years or even three years' worth of income in cash and, depending on how you feel about the future of the investment markets, that might be appropriate for you. This has the benefit of taking a lot of risk out of investing directly in the share market. For example, if you leave, say, 20 per cent of your investments in cash, then you reduce your level of risk by 20 per cent. You can vary this in line with your concerns about the future of the investment markets. When the economy is strong, you might feel optimistic and leave less money in cash and when the economy is weak you might put more money into cash. Alternatively, you might invest a chunk of money in annuities or managed funds to reduce your concerns about investing in the share market.

The catch is you will need to balance your desire to reduce the risk related to your investments and an expected fall in return with your income needs. The more money you put into low-interest-generating term deposits or annuities, the less income you will generate compared to putting more money into high-yielding listed companies. While it is tempting to take an extremely conservative stance and put a large chunk of money into cash, you need to think about this carefully, as it will undermine your portfolio's ability to generate income.

Investment markets are in a constant state of change and you need to keep a watchful eye out for these changes and try to anticipate them. Going back several years, it was possible to invest in term deposits and achieve a relatively strong rate of return in excess of 5 per cent. As those in retirement typically pay no tax on their income, 5 per cent after tax was largely seen as a good return, particularly as these deposits were bank guaranteed and so totally secure. The big downside of putting money into term deposits is there is no capital growth. If you invest large sums of money into term deposits you will slowly erode the buying ability of the savings you do have, so you need to be mindful of that.

At the time of writing, several of Australia's big miners are emerging as some of the best income-generating assets in the share market. This is a conscious decision made by their boards several years ago to trim their exploration budgets and focus on generating cash streams they can pay to their investors by way of dividends. In addition, they are refocusing their financial structures so they can pay those dividends fully franked. As these companies are also achieving strong capital gains in terms of their share price, they are becoming increasingly attractive to retirees.

The reason I mention this is that investing is an ever-changing activity. There are periods in the investment cycle when you are best advised to invest in low-cost managed funds, while there are other times when you are best advised to invest directly in the share market. In addition, the federal government in its wisdom is constantly changing the rules surrounding retirement savings. For example, annuity products were once exempt from Centrelink's assets test. This is no longer the case, and this prompted big changes in the way most retirees structure their financial affairs. At the time of writing there is some debate as to whether there should be changes made to the way franking credits are treated that may stop retirees receiving their big tax refunds once a year. If this proceeds it would prompt a major rethink concerning retirement strategies.

If this all sounds complicated, that alone is probably the best reason for finding a good financial adviser to help you as you move into retirement, and more importantly to ensure your savings remain well invested.

And don't skimp when it comes to other advisers

Just as it's important to have a good financial adviser by your side, you will also most likely need to have several other advisers you can call on as you need them. Having a good, caring accountant in the years before you retire is essential to help minimise your tax bill (by maximising your superannuation contributions) and ensure you have as much money in super as possible. All your long-term savings should be sitting within superannuation and once you retire you should establish an account-based pension, which will be paid to you effectively tax free. If your home and your superannuation are your only assets, you are receiving the Age Pension and/or an account-based pension, and your accountant does their work correctly in the years leading up to your retirement, you will never need to file a tax return again. You will forever live in your own tax haven!

At the same time, you will be well advised to find yourself a caring solicitor who specialises in helping clients prepare their wills. This can be a complex area, particularly if you are part of a blended family or feel there are members of your family who may dispute your will. A good solicitor can give you useful advice on how to minimise this possibility. Unfortunately, it is just part of modern Australia that more and more people die leaving a significant estate. They may have substantial savings in superannuation and an average family home in an Australian capital city can be worth more than one million dollars. With these larger estates comes the increased temptation for family members to dispute your will. While even a good solicitor can't ensure this doesn't happen, they can minimise the risk of it occurring.

Generating income and minimising risk

The key to retirement — regardless of the tax rules and Centrelink requirements around qualifying for the Age Pension — is to always maximise the income being generated from your investments while minimising the risk to the capital supporting that income.

This can be a moving target. It can, for example, largely depend on the prevailing tax rules. I find most retirees take advantage of the federal government's franking credit legalisation, which basically boosts by one-third the amount of dividend income generated by some companies. However, history shows that even a piece of law as deeply embedded as this can be questioned and subjected to review with the possibility of a future federal government revoking it.

It also depends on the prevailing market conditions. At the time of writing, term deposit rates are hovering between 1 and 2 per cent, which is basically the lowest they have been since World War II. This also goes for returns on residential property. It's possible over the next 40 or 50 years these market conditions will change and as a retiree living off your savings, you and your financial adviser will need to keep track of these changes.

More importantly, you will need to adjust your investment decisions accordingly. While it is possible to establish an investment strategy at the start of retirement, it is vitally important to review it during retirement and make changes when and if they are needed.

Your bottom line

You would think by the time most people reach retirement age they would be familiar with the concept of budgeting. And I know I have touched on this earlier, but it is such an important topic it's worth revisiting.

Budgeting can be a vexed matter. Some people do it easily and others struggle. It can be as simple as keeping an eye on your credit card balance each month, or it can be a detailed spreadsheet of where every last dollar went during the month. There are some great apps that can help with this and they vary as to how much detail they go into and how much they cost. Most of them take what's referred to as a direct feed from your bank accounts so there is no need to spend hours and hours entering your expenditure line by line into a spreadsheet.

Without at least a general idea of how much money you spend, you are setting yourself up for some big disappointments in retirement.

These can be extremely useful if you're the sort of person who gets to the end of the month never understanding where all your money went. Knowing what you spend your money on, of course, is extremely important in retirement. You want to enjoy life, but you should have a good idea of how much money you need on a week-to-week basis. This in turn will give you a solid understanding of how much income you need to generate in retirement to get by, so you can live within your means.

Without at least a general idea of how much money you spend, you are setting yourself up for some big disappointments in retirement. Either you will be too frugal and miss out on enjoying life to the full or you will spend too much and find yourself running out of money.

Making sure your retirement savings last throughout retirement involves firstly knowing just how much income you can safely generate from your investments and then knowing how much you need or like to spend and making sure you never spend more than your investments generate.

This is not as obvious as it seems. Potential clients came to see me some years ago concerned the value of their investments seemed to be constantly falling no matter what was happening in the share market. They couldn't understand why. They owned a portfolio of shares in good-quality companies paying high-yielding dividends that were all fully franked. They had a regular income stream based around the full value of the income being generated by their portfolio. Once a year they visited their accountant, completed their tax return and received the franking credits attached to the dividends back in the form of a cash refund. They used this not insignificant cash refund to finance their travels overseas. That seemed fine on the surface, but they were effectively double counting their franking credits. The income stream they had in place was based on the value of the dividends and the franking credits, but they never contributed those franking credits to the portfolio that supported their regular income stream. It was an easy mistake to make, but it meant they were spending more than their portfolio was earning for them by almost 50 per cent. They were reducing their capital each year by the amount they were overspending. This was fine for a few years, but it inevitably started showing up that the capital they were relying on to generate income throughout their retirement was being eroded by their level of spending. It was some tough medicine, but the answer was to stop travelling for a few years and rein in some other expenses to let their portfolio recover.

Never spend more money than your portfolio generates.

This, of course, is what it is like to live like a millionaire. You need to live within your means. No matter how large your pool of savings is, no matter how much money it is generating for you, you must ensure you spend less than your portfolio is generating, otherwise you will start eroding your pool of savings and generating even less money. This is the key plank in making sure your money lasts as long as you do in retirement. Never spend more money than your portfolio generates.

Your 'bucket list'

Once you've worked out your budget and how much your savings are likely to generate for you, how do you budget for one-off expenses? The 'bucket list' items. Those things you've spent a lifetime dreaming about: 'One day I'm going to own a soft-top sportscar/grand piano/painting by Pro Hart.' There's no denying they are there. The challenge is to squeeze them into your retirement plans without going broke or ending up on the breadline.

The place to start is by writing them all down over a period of, say, six months and then at the end of that time, coming back and prioritising the list in terms of which items are important to you and which are not.

When you've finished doing that, the next challenge is coming up with a dollar cost next to each item and again living with it for a while. Depending on how large your retirement savings are, you might find at this point you can go out and spend the next 12 months splurging and one by one ticking those items off your list and literally putting them in the trophy room.

For many, it will be a matter of sitting down, re-evaluating a few items and deciding which items are most important to you. There might be some items you can compromise on. You might buy that soft-top sportscar, but buy it knowing in four or five years you will sell it to top up your savings. But hey, it might be fun to have it just for those short years and you may even sell it at a profit, so perhaps when you step back and think about it there is little harm done to your retirement savings. Writing down these items is a crucial step if you want to own them without putting your overall plans in doubt. It will let you take control of the situation and move them from being rash actions to considered steps.

For some, their dream is to travel to a remote location. The challenge may be to find a way to do this and stay within your budget and usually, if you commit to it, there will be a way to get there. The trick is to find the balance between satisfying those long-held dreams, maintaining a sensible attitude to your retirement savings, and deciding just how much money you can use to splurge on these sorts of items and still stay financially secure through retirement.

Needless to say, you only live once. If you don't do some of these things now you will never do them, and at the end of the day the only point in having money is to enjoy it, so just where the balance lies regarding your bucket list will vary from person to person.

By thinking outside the square — by thinking through your options — maybe you can indulge in your passions, even if it means just owning something for a few years in retirement rather than for life and so not putting your financial future at risk.

Splurging

This is the tough one. Can I splurge in retirement? I usually say to clients, 'let's just wait and see what happens'. There is a whole body of retirement planning literature that looks at sequencing. This is where sometimes, more by luck than anything else, clients manage to retire and invest their funds in a company, a sector or an asset class and it just takes off in value. Happy days.

Against this, some people, through no fault of their own, retire at a time when markets move against them, taking the value of their investments down and, depending on the fall in value, it can take years and years to recover from these losses.

During the GFC, for example, share markets peaked in November 2007 and from there, steadily fell through to March 2009. For retirees who invested at the start of 2008 it was a brutal introduction to the share market.

By the end of 2011, as long as those clients hadn't sold their investments, even those who had invested at the start of 2008 had recovered most if not all of the paper losses they had experienced through those earlier years. For those who invested at the start of 2009 it was a very different experience. Their investments soared.

When it comes to splurging in retirement, the best advice is to wait for those moments when your investments do unexpectedly take off and make strong profits. For example, a few years back, Commonwealth Bank shares were trading well above $90 a share. This was an ideal time for clients to sell down their holdings, take some profits and splurge.

Having said that, it is important you let your capital base grow through retirement and allow it to keep pace with inflation. This can be difficult to manage and you might need help from a professional adviser, but this is the one proviso when it comes to splurging if you've had a good year in the markets. By all means take those profits and enjoy them. You only live once. But just be careful you don't go overboard and spend too much of the profits. You want to see the total balance of your investments increase from year to year before you go too crazy spending money.

Cutting back

Against this there will be times when money invested outside of term deposits will take a step down. This can be disappointing, but the key is not to panic. If you did your homework or got good advice and are confident of the underlying investments, they should come good with time. It's just a matter of being patient. This is part of the investment cycle and you will need to accept it as part of the task of managing your investments.

Ensure your investments support you through your retirement by never spending more money than the portfolio or investments generate on a year-to-year basis. You need to be mindful of this no matter how large or small your retirement savings are, particularly in the early years of retirement when it can be a bit of a guessing game as to whether your savings will generate sufficient income for you to live the lifestyle you want to maintain.

If there are a couple of years when the markets are down and for whatever reason your investments are not generating the expected level of income, the important step is to moderate your spending accordingly.

If your retirement savings are sitting within a superannuation fund, this will be easy to achieve as it is just a matter of reducing the account-based pension you are receiving. If your investments are outside super you will need to take steps to reduce the payments being made to you or alternatively, when payments are made, set aside a percentage each month or payment cycle to be reinvested.

It's just about being mindful that financial retirement is all about income and that the income from your investments may vary from year to year.

This can seem a bit grim at the outset, but it need not be. In the normal run of retirement, it may mean you don't travel that year, or you cut back on going out for lunch and maybe try your hand at having picnics. Again, it is very much a case of thinking how you can do things differently. Perhaps do them and still enjoy what you're doing but spend less money in the process.

If you can take this approach you will give your investments the breathing space they need to recover from the invariable downturns in investment markets, but you can do so with confidence that this is not a permanent thing.

The markets will recover, income levels will rise, and you will be able to get back to more normal spending patterns in the years ahead.

It's just about being mindful that financial retirement is all about income and that the income from your investments may vary from year to year. Most years this will be only a slight variation. Some years it will be bigger. By keeping attuned to how your investments are performing, and moderating your spending in years when they are generating less income, you will ensure you never spend more than you are earning and so will never erode your capital. That's how you can make sure your money will last as long as you do in retirement.

So, remember to ...

- *be mindful that the return on investment assets will vary from year to year.* You'll need to spend less than your investments generate. Living off your investment returns is very different from living off a wage or salary.

- *review your investments once a year.* A clever strategy if you have an account-based pension is to determine how much income your assets made in the previous 12 months and set your income for the next 12 months below this amount.

- *find a good financial adviser.* Moving into retirement is a complex step, and it pays to find a good financial adviser to help you make the most of your financial situation now and as you progress through retirement.

- *get your affairs in order.* Find a good accountant and a good solicitor to help you with this by hopefully lodging your last tax return and establishing a will that won't trigger arguments or disputes among the beneficiaries.

- *establish a budget.* In retirement you will develop a good feel for what you can and can't afford, but in the first few years, while you are still adjusting to living off your savings, it pays to have a budget of your expected spending habits.

- *keep your spending in line with your income.* Some years will be better than others and this might be when you splurge on a bucket list item, but there will also be years where you need to cut back and you should be prepared for that too.

Take a moment to ...

... write down the five most important questions you will ask your financial adviser.

Most professionals will hold the first meeting free of charge. Make sure you make the most of this opportunity to determine what services they can provide you and how much they will charge you.

_____

_____

_____

_____

_____

Chapter 6
Thrive in retirement

Retirement should be one of the most exciting times of your life. Embrace it. You might dream of spending more time with your family, particularly any grandchildren. You might have a closet passion you now have time to indulge and explore. You might want to chill and drop out of the 'hurley burley' of modern life. Whatever your vision, the biggest challenge is to simply enjoy it.

Having said that, it's hard to enjoy anything if you are worried or stressed by your financial situation, so your goal should be to achieve financial peace of mind. If you find yourself constantly stressing about money, you do need to find good-quality financial advice, and more importantly, listen to it.

Increasingly, Australians are entering a two-stage retirement and they need to plan for it. The first stage is where you are still relatively fit and active, and you should make the most of this. Don't fall into the trap of doing nothing the moment you stop working. This stage of retirement can last 10 to 20 years, which is a long time to be doing nothing. You need some structure to your day. The second stage is where you find yourself naturally slowing down. You will be less mobile but hopefully, if you've stayed fit and healthy, you will still be mentally alert and able to remain independent. It's unlikely you will be able to undertake any paid or unpaid employment, but you will have fewer financial needs.

In retirement, more than at any other time in your life, the only thing holding you back is yourself and the limitations you place on yourself.

During the earlier stage of retirement, though, it can be a big plus to continue earning money in some way. Not only will this help to keep you involved and engaged in your community, but it will also have a financial benefit. By earning a bit of extra money in the early years, you will reduce the income your investments need to generate for you and hopefully leave those funds in place to top up your savings. It can be a win–win situation. Look outside the square. Consider all the options available to you for earning money. Plunge in.

Retirement is a unique time because you can stand back and think through your options without any pressure. Most of our lives are spent responding to situations and opportunities. We don't get to choose the families we are born into and few of us get to choose the sort of education we experience. As we move into the workforce it's often a case of accepting the jobs offered to us and making the most of these opportunities. Before long most of us find ourselves married and with a family and this sweeps us along through a whole raft of experiences.

In retirement, more than at any other time in your life, the only thing holding you back is yourself and the limitations you place on yourself.

The other big plus of retirement is you've now reached an age where you have a better perspective on life. You can plan better and have realistic expectations of what you are able to achieve and how you would like to spend this final chapter of your life. Here are some ideas.

Start a business

Starting a business won't be on everyone's retirement list. If this is something you are keen on, you should absolutely try your hand. Age is no restriction to starting a business, nor should it restrict the size of the business you create. The biggest difficulty you will face is, if you've never run a business before there is a lot to sort through and understand, but then if you've never run a business before you won't be put off by the fact there can be so much involved in running a business. You might have to think hard before you embark on this idea, but it is full of possibilities.

There are all sorts of businesses you can create in retirement. It might be as obvious as consulting back to your old industry or profession; or it might be finding a way of commercialising a much-loved hobby or activity, either selling actual goods you make or selling classes helping other people to enjoy a hobby you are passionate about. It might be embarking on something you have no experience in and which you know little about. It is possibly something that has caught your attention and you would like to do.

The good news is modern technology makes it easy to establish a business and give it a professional face without spending much money. This is perfect for any business but particularly if you've never started a business before. You can easily go online and have business cards and business stationery created for a fraction of what it would have cost a few years ago. Likewise, you can go online and set up a webpage for free. What's more, you can access free tutorials about establishing the sort of business you're interested in and you can learn how to promote your business both on and off the internet without spending huge amounts of money.

Creating a new business can be an exciting time, and retirement can be the perfect time to try your hand at this. The big proviso is for you to keep a handle on how much money you devote to the business. It's tempting in retirement when you are sitting on a large pool of retirement savings to be blown away by the possibilities and invest a large slice of your savings into a new business venture. This can be a successful strategy for some, but for most people it's a recipe for financial disaster.

As a rule of thumb, you should expect to lose any money invested in a business. That's not being overly pessimistic, it's just being realistic and you should remember this whenever you are thinking of starting a business. The results of using your retirement funds to start a business are almost always disappointing. It can be hard to get a new business going and it can be easy to spend money on business-related activities and have very little to show for it.

What's more, operating on a tight budget can be a good discipline for any new business. It forces you to think of innovative ways to market your business and achieve your goals. The internet can make it cheap to get an idea up and running. If it really is a good idea, then the business should be able to generate the cash you need to keep it going within the first year or so. Whatever you do, don't risk putting a large chunk of your precious retirement savings into your new business venture unless you can see there is a solid market for what you are doing and, more importantly, that you can turn a profit.

Side hustles

Side hustles can be a truly fun aspect of retirement. If you do have a hobby or interest you enjoy, why not take it to the next level in retirement and in the process generate some income?

To me, a side hustle is not so much a business but something you enjoy doing that can generate a few dollars. Just as every hobby or interest is different, so are the ways you can make money from it. I have one client who successfully monetised his hobby and in doing so, found a way to finance his travels around Australia. He loves working in his shed during the winter months making kitchen items such as chopping boards and spice racks. He and his wife then spend their summer months touring Australia's regional areas. They plan their travels to coincide with local festivals and markets where he sells what he spent the winter making.

The benefits are endless. He and his wife choose exactly how much time and effort they put into this activity and they decide exactly where they will travel each year. It enables them to get out and about and not only do they meet new people when they sell their goods, but they make friends among the other market holders they work alongside. It's family friendly and weather friendly and most of all it's bank friendly.

They never tie too much money up in the business and they rely on the cash flow from the business to finance their travels, including updating their four-wheel drive every few years and paying for their accommodation, which is usually a caravan site. They also get to spend large chunks of time together doing something they both love. For them it's the perfect way to spend their retirement and is a dream come true.

This is just one way of making money from a hobby. Never tie too much money up in commercialising a hobby and aim to keep it flexible. A good retirement activity is one you can vary from one year to the next to fit around other family obligations that never makes you feel tied down or obligated. Retirement should be about having fun.

... the positives of running your own business in retirement far outweigh any potential reduction in pension entitlements.

Side hustles are best kept simple and straightforward. If you're not sure of all your obligations in starting a business, have a chat with a caring accountant. If the business's turnover is under $75 000 a year you will avoid such things as registering for the goods and services tax (GST). And you will need to declare the income both for tax purposes and for Centrelink purposes if you are receiving the Age Pension.

Don't let this thought stop you from creating a business. Just because you might lose a few dollars each week from your Age Pension entitlements is no reason not to try to expand your horizons. As long as you're not risking your hard-earned retirement savings, the positives of running your own business in retirement far outweigh any potential reduction in pension entitlements. What's more, as soon as you stop earning the extra money, your Age Pension entitlements will bounce back up. There is little to lose and a lot to gain from such a venture.

Make money from travelling

For many, the image of a perfect retirement, particularly in the early years, is to travel. However, the reality of their financial situation can be they just don't have the cash to finance the travels of their dreams and if they do, drawing down on those funds might put their financial position into jeopardy in later years.

Fortunately, there are lots of budget-friendly ways to travel and in choosing one of them, you can take some of the pressure off your retirement savings and help ensure they can finance you more effectively through retirement.

The obvious starting point is renting out your home while you are travelling. This means rather than it sitting empty while you're away, someone is living there and paying rent, which is generating a new source of income that can finance your travels. Some people will be horrified by the thought of having strangers living in their home, but others will see a real opportunity here.

So much so it might influence where you choose to retire. For example, you might sell your suburban home and buy a house on the coast knowing such a property will be sought after by holiday makers over the summer holidays as well as at other times during the year. You might choose to move to an inner-city apartment for the same reasons, although you will need to check you can rent out this type of property as a short-term rental with the body corporate manager.

It takes a bit of planning to ensure a property is suitable for tenants, and a local real estate agent should be able to provide you with advice. You will also need to make plans for storing your personal items while the property is being rented, although this might be as simple as putting a lock on the garage or a spare bedroom.

Or you might swap homes with a retired couple living in another state or country. There are several websites online set up to help with this. Think carefully about having strangers in your home, though. As with anything, there are pitfalls. However, it can be a great way of making friends around the world as well as securing low-cost accommodation as people who swap their houses usually stay in contact with each other.

Conversely, there are ways to make money that involve you travelling. One client of mine boosted his finances in retirement by working as a tour guide for a local bus company offering day tours to passengers visiting his local metropolitan city as part of their larger international cruise trip experience. He enjoyed getting out and meeting tourists from all over the world, while the company he worked for loved the fact he was so flexible with his time and was happy to do overnight tours. If they suddenly found they had more demand for a particular tour, they knew they could contact him at short notice and most likely he would be available to help them out. As he was retired, he was extremely flexible with his time.

There are similar opportunities to be had while travelling. If you travel overseas, you need to be mindful of any local rules or regulations that govern working while you are there. Ignorance is no defence, nor is claiming you're old and didn't realise the rules applied to you. Foreign authorities are unlikely to be swayed by this argument. There are endless possibilities; you just need to be positive and prepared to think creatively.

Write a book

Retirement frees you from the hustle and bustle of everyday working life and along with it (usually) the demands of family life, leaving you with plenty of time on your hands.

How you fill that time is up to you, but many people find the slower pace of life gives them the opportunity to breathe and reflect on life and achieve an inner calm that is ideal for writing a book. What's more, a book can take any shape or form and be literally about anything that interests you, or perhaps more importantly, if you want to be formally published, that might interest others.

Too often the stumbling block is worrying that you won't be successful. What if I don't finish it? What if it isn't any good? What if it's never published? And of course, the overwhelming answer is, who cares! If you feel the impulse to write, follow it.

Many people find the best part of writing a book is having the excuse to research a particular topic or interest and putting that research into a formal structure.

Ian Macfarlane, former governor of the Reserve Bank of Australia, has famously written two books since he retired. The second book, *Ten Remarkable Australians: They made their mark on the world but were forgotten*, was, he says, very much an excuse to research the lives of people he had stumbled over while reading Australian history books over the years and which he simply wanted to know more about.

Of course, you don't have to be a famous or successful Australian to spend your retirement writing books. Albert Facey, author of *A Fortunate Life*, shot to fame in the early 1980s, having just published an autobiography about his humble early beginnings. It was a straightforward account of his early years growing up in a very tough Western Australian country town and then serving as a private at Gallipoli. Its best features were the simplicity of his story and the honesty with which he told it.

Some of the best stories are never published. Family histories can be important stories and retirement can be the perfect time to put in the research to understand how your family got to be where it is.

There are endless topics to choose from when researching for a potential book, and who cares if you never finish it or publish it. The key is you are doing something that interests you and keeps your mind active. Too often in life, we become focused on the destinations or outcomes, when we should be looking at the journey or the process to justify what we are doing. Retirement is nothing if not about the journey. The destination is something you want to put off for as long as possible.

Start a blog

This might appear to be a small step away from writing a book, but there is an endless range of online activities you can turn your hand to when you're retired that can offer much the same challenge but with a more immediate response than writing a book.

The obvious choice if you are particularly interested in a hobby or activity is to start an online blog via a website, but of course it doesn't need to stop there.

You can create a community page on Facebook, for instance, and quickly gather around you a group of people who share your interests or beliefs. There are several online platforms that are as easy to use, immediate and flexible as Facebook. Take your time in finding the right platform for you.

And don't be put off by the technology. It's much easier and cheaper than you think. All you need is a cheap laptop, access to the internet and a smartphone, and the online world is literally yours.

Probably the best place to start is to go online yourself and start wandering around, looking at various topics of interest, and you will soon see opportunities where you too can add your voice to an online community.

It's all about being proactive and engaged and creating a sense of purpose and a community around you. You will be surprised just how many people on the internet share your interests and thoughts.

Go back to school

An exciting option for many retirees is returning to 'school': a university course or a short and simple online course — whatever you like.

There are now fee-paying obligations, which might make you think twice if you are trying to obtain a university degree, but don't be put off. If you are retired and unlikely to return to the workforce, why would you hesitate to take out a HECS debt, which you only need to repay if your taxable income reaches a certain level? Shop around. There are lots of options that might enable you to take much the same course: the University of the Third Age (U3A), which is a free online university service specifically targeting older mature-age students, is one example. There is also an endless range of TAFE courses and certificate-based courses that can help you develop a better understanding of whatever task or discipline has caught your attention. Some of these are free. This can even include learning a musical instrument or a foreign language. There is no pressure on you to achieve a certain standard, only to enjoy what you are doing in the here and now. Activities such as these have been found time and time again to boost cognitive function and stave off the likelihood of brain deterioration such as dementia in old age. This alone makes them worth doing, if you ask me.

A tree change

Retirement is very much a time for renewal and thinking about how you can enjoy every single day as much as possible, from the moment you wake up until the moment you fall asleep. That will mean different things to different people, but importantly you shouldn't be restricted by what you have done in the past or what your children or extended family might think you should be doing in the future.

One obvious option is moving to the country. This might mean buying a farm, having a bit of extra space or living in a suburban house in a small country town where it's easy to get around to do everything you need to do.

The big financial advantage of moving from a large city to a country location is typically you can buy a new home for a lot less than you will receive by selling your old home in town. That's not always true, but it is often the case. This doesn't mean you have to kiss life in the city goodbye. There's nothing like spending a weekend in town, enjoying the night life or visiting your children. It doesn't mean losing touch with loved ones or the community that's supported you in the past. For most, it just means opting for a quieter, easier pace of life.

It can also take a lot of pressure off you financially, especially since the federal government introduced 'downsizer' contributions. These allow those in retirement to sell their primary residence and contribute up to $300 000 each, or $600 000 for a couple, into their superannuation fund, where it can be used to generate a tax-free pension.

This is a great option. It means by selling the family home you can set yourself up for retirement, which can be attractive if you haven't been focused enough on retirement strategies. There is a trade-off as these funds will then be included as part of your assets test by Centrelink because they are in your super and no longer tied up in your home. It is something you should think through before you act on — and do get good advice on this before you make a decision. It can help boost your retirement savings and change your financial position from one of just getting by to one where you are financially comfortable in retirement.

A sea change

Conversely, a lot of Australians dream of moving to the beach and being able to wake up and go for a surf in the morning, and at the end of the day, falling asleep listening to the waves in the background. This is probably the opposite of moving to the country in every sense as most beachside homes are expensive, which will have a negative effect on your retirement finances. It might mean living somewhere that is quite busy and hectic, at least over the summer months, rather than slow and laid back.

Not all beachside homes are more expensive than the typical family home you might be selling in a capital city. This is where you will need to do your homework. Begin with a solid valuation on what your home is worth today and then shop around to determine what you might be able to buy on the coast. Again, it comes back to thinking outside the square. There is no end of coastline and beaches in Australia. You might have to start thinking of somewhere a bit further from home, or perhaps in another state, to realise your coastal dreams. In fact, you might have to think extra hard to make this happen, but there are a couple of things that may work in your favour.

If you find once you sell your house in town and buy a house on the coast you don't have much change, you will have the Age Pension to fall back on. While the federal government is likely to tinker with this in future years, remember that your primary residence is exempt from inclusion in the Age Pension assets test, so that's a big plus. You might find you're entitled to the Age Pension whereas previously you weren't.

There's another option too. Prime coastal real estate can bring in huge rental returns if rented out as a holiday let for a few weeks over Christmas and the school holidays. Perhaps you can work the numbers so while you rent your home out during these peak weeks, you take the opportunity to travel inland or find cheaper accommodation elsewhere.

You'll need to think this through and do the numbers — even if retirement means upscaling your family home, there might still be ways to make it work. Just pause and think.

Get fit!

The best retirement planning in the world is nothing if you don't stay fit, active and able to enjoy it. Regardless of your attitude towards personal fitness up until now, in retirement your focus should be on staying as fit and healthy as possible. There are no reasons for not doing this. While you were working you could get away with saying you didn't have time, but in retirement you can't.

It may be as simple as going for a walk first thing in the morning or you might take up weights or go to the gym for the first time. Surprisingly, the fact that you haven't paid much attention to staying fit in the past doesn't necessarily mean you can't get fit now or indeed tone up your body or lose those extra pounds.

Retirement is different these days from when your grandparents retired. Back in the day, people would retire and typically their health would slowly decline until they eventually passed on. What's more, most people passed on in their sixties or seventies. That's no longer the case. People can have quite serious medical issues in early retirement, only to receive medical treatment that resolves the problems and gives them a new lease on living. This, combined with 12 months of giving up cigarettes, not drinking and losing those extra pounds can change who you are.

Whatever health issues await you down the track, the healthier you are when you deal with them, the better the chances are that you will deal with them successfully and bounce back to having a great retirement.

Getting fit doesn't have to be expensive. Going for a walk every morning costs nothing. Consuming more vegetables and less alcohol will actually save you money. Both will create a better, fitter you. While getting your finances in shape is important, you can't expect to have a happy, lengthy retirement without paying attention to your health.

You don't need to go overboard and spend a fortune. You don't need to set up a home gym (although it is getting increasingly cheaper to build one if you want to). You don't need to turn into a gym junkie either, although you will have time for it. Greg Norman, Australia's renowned golfer, spends every morning working out in the gym and is more than happy to be photographed with his shirt off to prove it! So make sure staying healthy is part of the vision you have for yourself in retirement.

Get involved!

Report after report confirms that as you age it is incredibly important to get involved: be involved in family and as part of your community and force yourself to get out.

Being involved can come about in various forms. The most obvious is volunteering in your local community. I had a client whose retirement was sorted, so he 'works' at volunteering for various community groups five days a week, 40 weeks of the year, and by all accounts he enjoys every minute of helping with activities from sailing to handing out food rations. His only criteria for volunteering is that he can take time off when he wants to go travelling and when he wants to be available for his family.

It keeps him fresh, engaged and alert and it allows him to maintain a regular rhythm to his life. You might find this too much like being back in the workforce, but it does show what you can do to ensure you enjoy your retirement, however you define it.

Think of new ways of getting involved. Don't be restricted by what you define as 'family'. There will be lots of young families in your neighbourhood that don't have active grandparents close by or in their lives and would love to have a spare pair of hands from time to time to help with their family duties. You might volunteer a bit of free babysitting if you feel able, or just wander around and bring in the odd garbage bin for a neighbour who you can see is under pressure sprinting from work to home and getting the children to school and generally having a hard time of it.

There's no shortage of families or groups needing an extra hand and there's no better way to feel a part of things than giving of yourself and helping others in life. It will help you thrive in retirement.

So, remember to ...

- *find a new mojo*. Few people stop working completely at age 65. Find a side hustle, volunteer or turn a hobby into a business — you just need to find your groove.

- *consider starting a business*. Maybe you've always had a great business idea sitting in the back of your mind or maybe it's only just occurred to you. As long as you keep a close eye on the dollars and don't risk too much money, retirement can be the perfect time to see if you can make it work.

- *think through your travel plans*. If travel is important to you and you're on a tight budget, step back and consider your options. There are ways you can make money while you travel, and they could be easier and more enjoyable than you think.

- *keep mentally fit*. Think about going back to school. Find a course that interests you, take up a musical instrument or learn a new language. There are so many free online courses for attending university as a mature-age student. The possibilities are only limited by you. And the benefits to your mental health are enormous.

- *keep physically fit*. There is every chance you will live for 30 or 40 years in retirement, which will only be fun if you stay physically fit. Just as you would never dream of going through the day without brushing your teeth or having a shower, make it a rule you will do some form of physical exercise every single day.

- *think about where you want to live*. Just moving to the beach or to the country will change your life and open up new opportunities and challenges. It doesn't mean you have to live there forever, but why not spend the first half of your retirement somewhere new? Perhaps you can rent your home out for a few years and rent somewhere different. Focus on enjoying life.

Take a moment to ...

... write down the things you've always wanted to do and never found the time for.

Retirement is your time to do those things you've always dreamed of. When you're retired and you're asked, 'What do you do all day?', the right answer is always 'Exactly what I want to do!'

_____

_____

_____

_____

_____

_____

Chapter 7
Families: love 'em and leave 'em

Usually, when people reach retirement age they find they are financially comfortable — and that's a great thing. It means you've worked hard all your life and you've put away sufficient funds to provide for yourself in retirement. Retirement should be a time to relax and enjoy your life and family. Sadly, the best-laid plans can go astray and the cause can be the people who love you most: your family.

Family members are quick to notice that if you are able to provide for yourself in retirement, you must have a stash of cash somewhere. The temptation, then, for family members is to 'relieve' you of some of that cash. This plays on the natural parental instinct to provide for and help your children. The cash is there, within easy reach...your children have a need...and so you draw down a percentage of your retirement savings. It's so easy. It's so tempting. *It's so bad. It should be resisted at all costs.*

Focus on what giving away a chunk of cash might do to you and your chances of successfully funding your retirement right to the end. Think about the final years of your life and what it would mean if you ran out of money and only have the Age Pension to rely on. It's a situation you wouldn't enjoy and you'd enjoy it even less if you knew the reason you're in that situation is because of decisions you made earlier in retirement to give your children a bit of financial help that they might not even remember.

To be forewarned is to be forearmed, so in this chapter I will run through the more common traps. This may not stop your family from taking advantage of you, but hopefully you will make better decisions in terms of helping family members out financially and so minimise the adverse impact doing so might have on your retirement.

Of course, none of this applies if you own considerable assets when you retire and can afford to give away chunks of money. The challenge then is to transfer some of your assets to your children in a way that is fair and transparent so if you have several children, none of them feels overlooked or slighted. This can be a difficult road to tread. If you have a caring family solicitor, you should involve them to ensure your wishes are abided by when you pass on.

A good solicitor will alert you to the risk of helping your children financially and then later finding them caught up in a financial crisis such as an acrimonious divorce. You might, in good faith, give or lend money to a child to help them pay off or reduce their mortgage only to discover their former partner is entitled to the family home and other assets paid for with your money.

Even if you have significant savings in retirement, tread carefully before you start handing cash to your children. Think before you act and get good legal advice. Ensure you tell all your children what you are doing in a fair and transparent way very early on or you might lay a minefield the family walks through at every family gathering thereafter.

The cost of education

Australians are marrying and starting families later in life. While parents starting second families in their late fifties and early sixties remain an exception, it is common for retirees to have children in tertiary education.

Unless your child has been lucky enough to secure a scholarship to university, they will be paying for their own education and most likely will incur a HECS debt. Many parents feel the urge to pay these debts, but

Whenever you might be tempted to pay your children's debts, think again.

unless you have significant assets set aside for retirement — and by that I mean millions of dollars each — you should refrain from doing this.

Dipping into your retirement savings to pay children's HECS debts can open a door to your precious retirement savings that can be extremely hard to close. Once your children sense there is a stack of money sitting somewhere and that with a bit of pressure they can get hold of some of it, doing so will quickly become a habit. This goes against all the best tenets of good parenting, which say you should encourage your children to stand on their own two feet both financially and emotionally.

It also means your finances will be discussed at the family meal table and at other social occasions when it is clearly not appropriate to do so. It will become a nuisance and will slowly build from being a petty annoyance to something that regularly starts arguments and disharmony in your family. Whenever you might be tempted to pay your children's debts, think again. Having seen more than one family implode over these sorts of financial issues, I can tell you it's not worth it. It's particularly not worth it over a HECS debt. Of all the debts your children might incur, this is the one you should encourage them to face up to and pay.

For many, it will be their first taste of a financial obligation. Owning the debt will encourage them to prize their education, ensure they make the most of it and not hop from one tertiary course to another. It's also an important step for them to recognise they are part of a wonderful country and have a social obligation to give back as successful young adults.

So, as tempting as it is to help out with a HECS debt, you should avoid this, especially if it means dipping into your retirement savings. If you choose to stay in the workforce and work, say, an extra year to pay off your child's debt, that's another thing altogether. That's your choice, and it won't adversely impact your retirement. In fact, such a decision will help improve your financial position in retirement as you will have another year of contributions in your super account.

Helping children buy a house

Next on the list of activities that can easily undermine your plans to fund your retirement is helping your child buy a home or, if they are already in a home and paying a mortgage, reducing the burden of that debt. This can become a pressing issue if that child finds themselves in financial difficulties. It can be hard not to step in and help. Again, you should resist the temptation.

Buying a house is a big financial responsibility and too often Australians think it is a guaranteed way to make money. It's not. Even buying your own home can be full of difficulties and you need to be really committed to make it work. Encouraging a child to take on the responsibility of owing hundreds of thousands of dollars if they are not ready to do so is in many ways setting them up for failure. In fact, in some situations I've witnessed, I've wondered if that was the parent's intent: to set the child up for failure just so the parent can swoop in and rescue them down the track. That sounds a bit cynical, but there you are. It can be a means of tethering a child closely to you, which might make you feel good but is unlikely to do much for your child.

If you are determined to help your child buy a property, here are some suggestions. Encourage your child to take responsibility for their financial situation by saving the deposit. This might seem like a huge amount of money in today's property market but at no time in the past 100 years has it been easy for an average Australian to buy a home, and in fact it is no more difficult today. There are several ways you can encourage your child to save a solid deposit. Perhaps your child can live with you rent free. If you take this option, make sure they realise you are effectively helping them buy their home by providing them with free accommodation. It should be appreciated and they should help you around the house.

Another option is to match their savings dollar for dollar, but only if you believe you can afford to do so.

You should avoid going guarantor on the loan at all costs. Going guarantor basically makes you liable for the debt and, depending on the terms of the guarantee, you might have little control over the situation or how you can resolve it to your best advantage. If you must go down this route, there are now clever mortgage products on the market where you can co-tenant or be a part-owner in a property. This gives you much more control over what happens if your child finds they can no longer afford the payments. Another strategy is to place a second mortgage on the property.

Whatever you decide, make sure you talk to a caring lawyer first who can suggest ways to protect your interests if things go wrong. Above all else, make sure your actions are transparent. What you do for one child you must do for them all, unless you have a good reason for favouring one over the others, such as caring for a severely disabled child.

If you do decide to give a child a large sum of money and you are not prepared to involve a lawyer to put in place the necessary paperwork to safeguard your funds, then look upon it as a gift. Even if you and your child might see it as a loan, without formal documentation to confirm it's a loan, it is a gift — and trying to treat it as anything else will only cause family arguments. It's just not worth it.

Help them without stressing

We've seen when and how not to help your children with education and house costs. Now let's look at ways of helping them without ruining your budget or causing family tensions.

So your child has sent their children to private secondary schools and there is pressure on you as a grandparent to pay the fees for their final couple of school years because your child, for whatever reason, can no longer afford to pay. It can be difficult to say no, but it's best to speak to a solicitor before making any decisions. Certainly you would want to step in to ensure your grandchildren don't go through the upheaval of changing schools, and that's okay if you can afford it. But don't be tempted to be kind if the grandchildren are in primary school without involving a lawyer in your decision as it's a very long-term financial commitment. If you do provide financial support for their education, ensure you always have visiting rights to the grandchildren. Take steps from the very beginning to ensure that if you do make a financial contribution, you expect to always be able to see that child. There is nothing more hurtful for a grandparent who has paid for an expensive private education to later find they are cut out of the picture and can't attend school ceremonies, for example. And trust me, this happens. Ensure all your children know which grandchildren are receiving your financial support and equalise this gift by adjusting your estate planning wishes accordingly. Don't think you will be able to keep something like this a secret. Your other children will eventually find out and could be quite hurt if you haven't already explained the situation to them.

There are also better ways to help your children buy a property than just handing over cash. If you have a child who is married with children and, due to sickness or unemployment, is facing hard times, it can be tempting to step in and repay the mortgage for them, but this can lead to a litany of difficulties. It doesn't address the underlying problem, nor does it encourage your child to get back on their feet by their own means and in their own time.

Most damning is that it encourages children to think they can't cope with life's problems and continue to rely on you for help. A better solution is to contribute to the mortgage repayments, either entirely or partly, for a period of time to take the direct financial pressure off them. This solution means you are in the driving seat and you can stop making contributions at any time. Most importantly, you haven't just lost a big chunk of your savings and so undermined your own ability to generate income in future years. Nor will you ever face the difficulty of trying to get this money back.

And remember, as a grandparent and parent your primary role is to be there for moral support and to help where you can. Avoid providing financial support just because you have access to your superannuation savings or you could open a Pandora's box.

Caring for your parents

Caring for your parents can be even more distressing than caring for your children because elderly parents can seem so vulnerable and helpless in their final years. Again, you need to think carefully about the type of help you provide and how you are going to finance this help in the long term.

Australia's social security system provides support for people as they move to the final stage of their lives. There are many local government services you can take advantage of to help your parents stay in their own home for as long as possible. In these situations, the real help you can provide is not financial but dealing with the avalanche of paperwork they will face gaining this assistance.

A good option to consider for your elderly parents is a granny flat in your garden. This has a lot of merit. Parents can maintain independence and, if it is set up correctly, they should still be able to retain their Age Pension entitlements. The rules are complex, especially if it involves selling the family home, so contact Centrelink to discuss your options before making any decisions.

If your parent is living on the Age Pension and they need to progress into a nursing home, you are probably best to let the system take care of them. The cost of living in a government-run nursing home would be largely covered by their Age Pension entitlements. It's easy to look down on some of these establishments and compare them unfavourably to privately owned, expensive nursing homes. It's hard to take the emotion out of the decision. Just how good their quality of life in any nursing home will be is often more dependent on the person's immediate family and how supportive they are in terms of visiting and making sure the small comforts of life are on hand. This is usually more appreciated than being in a new facility with all the mod cons.

If you are tempted to reach into your retirement savings to pay for better care for your parents in their own home, think carefully. Often children do this with the expectation that when Mum or Dad passes on the money spent on their care will be returned to them from the sale of the family home. That's okay if you are an only child. If you have siblings, you will want to discuss it with them first to ensure they agree this expense should be paid from the estate when the time comes. They might disagree with you and see the money as a gift from you to your parents, that it has nothing to do with the estate and that you are only entitled to your share of the estate as set out in the will. This sort of unpleasantness can tear families apart at a time when they should be coming together. Best avoid this risk by making sure you speak with the other beneficiaries of the estate and if you expect to receive any additional funds, make sure you have it in writing in a legally binding format before you spend any money.

Passing on a business

I could easily justify writing a whole book on this topic. While I will only skim through the main issues, I thought I should include it for completeness. Passing on a business to the next generation can be full of pitfalls and obstacles, although the obvious joy of handing over a business — particularly one handed down to you from your parents — can be wonderful. Family businesses are usually established for the financial and general enjoyment of their owners. If your child or children are keen to take over the family business and they appear to have the skills to do so, that's great and it should be encouraged. But it should never be assumed or forced upon the next generation just because you think it's a good idea.

Start early in getting the next generation involved. Employ an outside consultant to oversee the process so it stays on track and ensure everyone in the family is happy with the decisions made. You might spend a lot of time sitting around a table talking, but it's important, if the business is to pass successfully from one generation to the next, that you take your time to do it properly. How this transition is undertaken will vary from family to family and business to business. If you are relying on the 'sale' of the business to finance your retirement, you will need to structure it so you get a reasonable price. By running your own business, depending on the nature and size of the firm, you will have some flexibility around how the business can be passed down to the next generation.

Get someone from outside the family, and preferably a specialist, to value the business and put the valuation out there for the whole family to see. If you have more than one child, it is important that every child is aware of the valuation and the decisions that will flow from it.

In planning your retirement, you don't have to bargain on getting the full value of the business or the agreed price for it in one hit. There are many ways a business can be passed on so everyone in the next generation feels they get a fair share of that inheritance. It may be some family members don't want to or can't be involved with the business. That's okay. It's not even necessary to make sure everyone gets an equal share. What's important is everyone is aware of the business's true value, why it is being passed on in the way it is and how their interests have been protected.

There are endless possibilities for how the business can finance your retirement. You might stay on the payroll in a non-executive role and receive a salary while doing little if any work. However, be aware that this risks you being left with no income and no retirement savings if sometime down the track, rather than selling the business and using the funds to finance your retirement, the business goes bust and you are left with nothing to sell. And it is a big risk. A better alternative is where you own the business premises and you pass the operating business on to the next generation. You can receive the rental paid on the premises to finance your retirement with the added safeguard if anything happens to the business and it goes bust, you have the premises to fall back on. You then have the option of reletting or selling the premises to finance your remaining retirement.

Depending on the size of the business, there may be ways it can continue to pay you. You may retain ownership of the business and receive income via dividends and effectively pass the day-to-day running of the business on to your child or children, who would, of course, receive a salary. There's still the concern the business might go bust and you will be left with nothing, but if you do see the business being mismanaged you can step in at any time and sell it. You effectively have control.

At the other end of this spectrum, you might sell the business outright to a child and receive a lump sum, several lump sums or a steady repayment of the amount owing throughout your retirement. Until the debt is completely paid, you could still retain ownership and with that be able to step in if things go wrong.

Start early. Get professional help to ensure the transition is as smooth as possible and when you reach a final agreement, spend the money to create a watertight agreement. This will help reduce arguments about what was or wasn't intended. Legal contracts can't foresee every eventuality but they can clarify your intentions in passing across the business. If there is a dispute down the track, referring to this document could well be the simplest way of ensuring any issues are quickly rectified.

Helping children buy a business

Never, ever, ever give money, lend money or guarantee a loan for a child who wants to use the funds to buy a business. If I didn't make that clear enough the first time around, let me write it again: Never, never, never give money, lend money or guarantee a loan to a child who wants to buy a business.

If they want to start their own business, great. This is where parental encouragement can come into its own. You might even extend some start-up capital in the way of a few thousand dollars, but no more. Even if you have significant retirement savings, you should never think of parting with any of it to help a child start a business, much less buy a business. And there is a big difference between the two. When starting a business, the amount of capital involved is meagre. Starting a successful business largely depends

Never, never, never give money, lend money or guarantee a loan to a child who wants to buy a business.

on sweat equity — that is, how hard your child is prepared to work to get that business up and running.

Buying a business can be worthwhile, but it's almost always a short cut. Rather than doing the hard yards required to establish a business yourself, you leave it to someone else and when they are exhausted or fed up and want to sell, you come in and often pick up a viable business at a good price. Alternatively, you might be completely misled and buy a business that is barely profitable and has little chance of becoming profitable. Either way, if you are using your own money and are happy to take the risk of buying a business, that's your call.

If owning their own business is your child's passion and they decide to achieve this by using someone else's money — specifically their parents' retirement savings — then you should see red lights flashing. Not only are they saying they are not prepared to put in the hard yards, but they are also not prepared to risk using their own money to buy the business. There's no way such a venture will end happily. For the sake of your family's long-term harmony, ignore any suggestion from any of your children that you could finance them into a business using your superannuation. Just close the door. Walk away.

If what I have written hasn't put you off lending your child money to buy a business, then at least keep this one thought in your head: any money you extend to a child to buy a business should be considered a gift. Okay, you might dress it up as a loan. You might even call in the lawyers to formalise an agreement that shows the monies are extended as a loan. At the end of the day, though, you most likely won't get anything back if the business goes bust and your child can't repay the loan.

Just as I suggested earlier with regard to helping out with a mortgage, as long as you think of the money as a gift, everything will be fine. If your child makes a success of the business and manages to repay the loan, fantastic. You can all go out and celebrate. If the business goes bust and your child can't repay the loan, it's merely an expensive lesson. You didn't expect the loan to be repaid, so you won't be disappointed. It can be written off as the price of family harmony.

Divorce dilemmas

Divorce can hit anyone in a married relationship at any time. It can even hit you if you're in a long-term de facto relationship and have tried to keep your assets separate. It can be completely unexpected or much anticipated and overdue. It can impact you personally at any stage in your life and it can impact your children's lives. There's not much you can do to avoid it except hope to minimise its effect on your retirement.

While you might suffer a divorce in retirement, let me focus first on how your retirement might be impacted if one of your children divorces. With 40 per cent of all Australian marriages ending in divorce there is a good chance this could happen. The best advice anyone can give you is to be prepared for the possibility of a child divorcing and to take simple steps to protect yourself and your finances.

First, stand back. This is not your problem and while it is tempting to ride in like the cavalry to fix any financial problems that might have brought the marriage to the edge, that's not your role. Nor is it your role to take sides, no matter how grievous you might find the situation or how appalled you are by the behaviour of either party. Your role is to provide love and support to both sides if possible.

This is particularly the case if there are children — your grandchildren — caught in the middle. Children need all the comfort they can get and as a grandparent you are in a perfect position to offer them support, even if they don't end up living with your child. In fact, the prospect your grandchildren may end up in the full custody of your child's partner makes it even more important you don't take obvious sides through a divorce.

Limit any discussions about finances and under no circumstances discuss family finances in front of your grandchildren.

Keep the prospect of divorce, no matter how unlikely you think it might be, front and centre of your mind should you ever 'lend' or 'gift' money to your children. And if it is a loan, ensure there is a legal document confirming this. If everything falls apart you might be very disappointed to find money you loaned your child become part of the matrimonial pool of assets.

Some people find themselves divorced or divorcing in retirement, and that can be devasting for some and a great relief for others. As hard as it may be, try to keep emotion out of it and make the break as quick and clean as possible. If there are no dependent children involved and the marriage has been successful for a long period of time, such as 20 or 30 years, you will need to split your total assets in half. Try to work this out between yourselves. That way, at least you will have some say over which assets go where. If you can't, the matter will go before the Family Court where a judge will decide for you.

Try at all costs to avoid involving lawyers. They do little more than stir up issues and add to the cost of separating. Even where modest assets are involved, it will be nothing for each party to incur legal fees of $150 000 each if you choose to use lawyers. That's $300 000 that will not be available to either of you. Sometimes the situation is so difficult there's no option other than involving lawyers, but again my advice is to try everything you can to settle the financial situation without them.

Grandchildren

While it is tempting to give money to adult children, it seems it is even more tempting to give money to grandchildren. If you want to live a long and happy retirement where you can pay your own bills and enjoy life without worrying too much about where the money is coming from, then don't give money to your grandchildren.

There is usually room in any budget to find $100 for a birthday gift or Christmas present. That's fine. Some grandparents decide for reasons of their own that they want to set up accounts with money or shares or some other investment in their grandchild's name. This is nearly always a mistake. It's difficult to invest any reasonable amount of money in a child's name and not have those earnings hit by high income taxes, and there are few children who appreciate paying higher taxes than they otherwise need to.

Children usually find this out when they get a job at a local supermarket and do their first tax return at age 15 or 16. While the other kids they work alongside all year will get a handy tax refund on their earnings, these grandchildren find they don't because Granddad bought shares in their name 10 years ago and didn't tell them. So they are hit with higher taxes even though they have never seen the shares or the dividends. It can be a difficult situation and makes little financial sense.

There is room for moderation. There is always a good argument for a grandparent to help financially if for some reason their grandchild is missing out in an irreversible way due to a shortage of funds. One example is that of a grandchild who is doing well at a private school and whose parents can no longer afford to pay the fees, as we saw earlier in the chapter.

The same goes if a child is particularly gifted or sporty and needs extra training or where a grandchild is sick and needs extra care. Few grandparents would hesitate to help financially in these situations.

Under any other circumstances, my advice is to keep your retirement savings intact. Don't spread money around because you think it will make you look like a wonderful grandparent or because you think your family will be extra appreciative. In my experience retirees rarely benefit by giving money away to family members. So it's best to keep it in your pocket unless it is really needed.

Dependent children: what to do

Some children will always need financial support, and this is a difficult situation. A child might have a minor disability and be less able to provide for themselves financially or they may have a serious disability and will need significant care throughout their lives. And there are many possible scenarios in between.

Seek good advice, not just from a financial planner but also from a caring solicitor, to come up with a good solution. Thankfully, the National Disability Insurance Scheme is available, which takes some financial strain out of these situations.

To help, the federal government has put in place provisions for parents to establish special disability trusts. Under these rules, parents can 'gift' up to $500 000 to contribute funds to a trust. As well, the principal beneficiary has up to $694 000 in assets within the trust exempted from any assets test for social security purposes. Setting up such a trust is complex and you will need to consult with a financial planner or lawyer. Think of yourself first and make good decisions that provide for your financial security. This can be extremely hard to do, especially after a lifetime of putting your child's interests first, which is what most parents of a child with a disability do. Life will be difficult enough as you grow old and try to care for your disabled child. Don't make it harder by undermining your own financial security if you can possibly avoid it.

Be completely honest with your other children about what you are doing. It might be a difficult conversation to have, but the best way forward is to get all your feelings out on the table. If it is going to be an emotional conversation, then maybe do it in the office of your financial planner or solicitor. Make sure everyone in the room has an opportunity to speak and, more importantly, that everyone feels they have been heard. Once the conversation has been had and the decisions made, it should not be referred to again. If you don't make that ruling and enforce it, there is every chance the conversation will re-assert itself in the future and typically at a time when family emotions are running high due to other events.

As long as you have taken time to think about it and sought good professional advice, you should be confident you are making the right decision. Hopefully your other children will be fully accepting and supportive.

Protect yourself from elder abuse

While the term 'elder abuse' is new, the concept isn't. Parents have been wanting to help their children and children have been accepting that help for time eternal. In fact, children have been pressuring their parents into helping them since time began. Nothing new there!

What is new is the growing number of older parents finding themselves sitting on family homes worth several millions or with retirement savings worth several millions. For a child desperate to make a mark on the world, these funds can prove too tempting to resist. Sadly, elder abuse, where parents are put under undue pressure to give financial help to their children, is here to stay and you might need to guard yourself against it.

Financial abuse is any situation where there is the illegal or improper use of a person's property, finances or other assets without their informed consent or where consent is obtained by fraud, manipulation or duress. Financial abuse may involve a family member taking a loan with the promise of repaying it but not paying the money back, straight out stealing, forcefully encouraging wills to be changed, or selling or transferring property without proper consent.

National Ageing Research Institute of Seniors Rights Victoria data suggests more than 80 per cent of older Victorians have suffered financial abuse and/or psychological/emotional abuse. Victims are more likely to be female and the perpetrators are mostly male. Persons related to the older person or in a de facto relationship with them account for almost all the abuse. More than half of all elder abuse is perpetrated by a child of the older person.

Elder abuse can happen at any time and sadly it becomes more common the further into retirement people are as they find themselves vulnerable to pressure. Take steps to avoid it. If there is a possibility of this happening to you, talk about it with your financial planner or with your solicitor — ideally with both.

Government bodies can also help should you believe you are the victim of elder abuse. Often it is the people you are closest to and who you least suspect of wanting to take advantage of you who do exactly that.

Love your family, but don't let them take advantage of you.

So, remember to ...

- *love 'em and leave 'em.* Families can be a great source of happiness as you get older but they can be a massive financial strain if you let them. It can start off with relatively modest amounts of financial assistance but this can quickly grow.

- *let your children stand on their own two feet.* It can be tempting when you find yourself suddenly managing a large pool of retirement savings, to dip into it and give some to a child. At every point, try not to do this.

- *ignore your children's financial situations.* Their debts and their financial problems are not your financial problems. Wherever possible, don't discuss your financial position with your children and discourage them from discussing their financial situation with you.

- *take your time when it comes to caring for your parents.* Just being present in their lives will mean so much more to them than any amount of money you might spend on them. Remember these precious retirement savings have to last you a long time.

- *get good advice if you are dealing with a business.* Whether you are selling a business to a child, passing it on to a child or trying to help a child start their own business, be very circumspect. Get good advice and protect your financial position at every turn.

- *view divorce as potentially the great wealth killer.* Divorce and separation can strike at any time in your life or in your children's lives. Again, get good advice and protect your financial position as much as you are legally entitled to.

- *consider all your options if you need to support a child throughout life.* This can be a very difficult and stressful situation. There are steps where you can help your child and ensure they maximise their own social security entitlements. Make sure you get good advice before you do anything to help a dependent child.

- *protect yourself from elder abuse.* This is sadly a very real and growing phenomenon in modern Australia and you should make yourself aware of the key warning signs that you might be at risk. Happily, more and more agencies and financial institutions are aware of this problem and can step in to help you at any time.

Take a moment to ...

... remind yourself that your children's financial problems are not your financial problems.

Write the names of the people in your life who you trust and who you believe you can turn to if you feel you are being put under unfair pressure to provide financial support.

_____

_____

_____

_____

_____

Chapter 8
Sexually transmitted poverty

A Husband Is Not a Retirement Plan: Achieving economic security for women in retirement is a federal government Senate report into the fate of Australian women who retired in 2016. It is very insightful.

It paints a bleak outlook for women. Men, on average, retire with twice as much super as women, while women, particularly single women, are at much greater risk of experiencing poverty, housing stress and homelessness in retirement. Grim stuff! So grim, it warrants a review of the unique issues facing women — and men — who reach retirement without much money in super.

Why women are particularly vulnerable

Women can find themselves in poor circumstances in their later years for a variety of reasons. They spend their lives in the workforce usually earning less than men. They spend prolonged periods out of the workforce, looking after their family, and during these periods, completely miss out on contributing to super. They often choose part-time work, and this further reduces their ability to make super contributions. All of these factors work against them building significant super balances.

In addition, many women avoid talking about their finances with anyone! This is weird, as survey after survey shows when women do get involved and take control of their financial situation, they prove to be much better managers than men — borrowing less, repaying debts more quickly and if they embark on their own business, their start-up success rate tends to outpace that of their male counterparts. How does it all go so wrong?

Too often, women simply avoid the issue of their finances generally, and specifically superannuation. If they are married, they tend to leave it to their husbands. That might be a good strategy — until they suddenly find themselves divorced. They can then feel completely lost, alone and overwhelmed by a dismal sense that it's all too late and unable to question their ex-husbands about their joint financial situation. Paradoxically, there is the possibility that if the wife had had input, different financial decisions would have been made resulting in vastly improved financial circumstances. Few men like to be outdone on this front.

There is also no denying, as much as it might not be politically correct to say so, that many single women hope a special person will enter their lives and bring with them financial security. They drift through life with this often unacknowledged hope, and when they reach retirement age and find this hasn't happened, they are overwhelmed by a sense of despair that it's all too late.

As I say to my clients, while it is never too early to think about retirement planning, it is also never too late. No matter how hopeless you think your financial situation might be, it is always worth getting good advice and acting on it. There are always opportunities to either extend your working life — no matter how unpalatable it might seem — and so boost your retirement savings, or to do more with the assets you have. It's all about taking stock of where you are now and finding the best way forward.

Get sympathetic advice

As a financial planner, it might sound self-serving for me to argue that women in particular should seek out financial advice, but it's so important. It's not that women can't manage their affairs. It's just that, in my experience, most don't and so they lack confidence when they try to. Women, generally more than men, do need to find a good financial adviser who they understand and trust and who will act in their best interests.

This is a big step for most women. Inevitably, they think if they speak to a financial adviser, they will be embarrassed or be made to feel they should know much more about financial issues than they do. However, when you think about it, that is a nonsense.

Financial planners spend a large chunk of their working lives helping people who don't know much about financial matters — and that's exactly why. Most people only have a superficial understanding of finances. It's a bit like suggesting you are not going to see your doctor because you're embarrassed you won't know as much about medicine as they do. Or thinking your doctor expects you to be as well versed about physical ailments as they are. That would be absurd. And yet I hear time and time again from women they don't want to talk to a financial planner, either male or female, because they fear they will be made to look stupid. Put that aside and accept you could benefit from the advice they can give you.

The other issue holding people back is they fear they don't have enough money to justify meeting with a financial planner. Again, this is a nonsense. The fact you don't have much money makes it even more important you get good advice to help you make the most of the financial resources you do have. A good financial planner will help you protect the funds you have so you don't fall foul of some of the more obvious investment pitfalls.

Female clients also tend to try to justify how they got themselves in the position they are in and explain why they have made the investment decisions they have. That's okay if your purpose is to give the financial planner a better understanding of who you are and your attitude towards investing. It's not okay though, if you use it as a defensive argument not to change anything about your investments.

If your investments were sorted, you wouldn't be speaking to a financial planner in the first place. And if a financial planner thought your financial affairs were in order and they couldn't help to bring any value to your life, they would be honest and tell you so. However, it is rare for anyone to have their finances so well sorted an adviser can't improve their circumstances.

The truth is it's difficult to retire in Australia and make the most of your financial situation without professional advice. Rather than showing the world you're not very smart, seeking out the advice of a caring financial planner is the clever thing to do. If you don't feel you are comfortable dealing with the first financial planner you meet, shop around. The onus is on the financial planner to make you feel comfortable and show you how they can help improve your financial outcomes in retirement.

The challenges

Many women cry off from looking after their financial affairs by saying they are not good with numbers. That's just not good enough. As you prepare for retirement, especially if you are alone, you need to focus and understand how you are going to finance your retirement in a way that will make it sustainable for as long as you live.

Understanding your investments should not be hard, particularly if you make the smart decision of employing a caring financial planner. Part of their role is to make sure you understand the key elements of your financial affairs. If you choose not to employ a financial planner, at least make sure you understand all the options being offered to you by your superannuation fund.

Most super funds hold information nights where they explain what your options are in terms of establishing an account-based pension or regular income stream, and you should make the effort to attend them. Every seminar you attend will increase your understanding and gradually you will start to make sense of things.

Every superannuation fund has an enquiry line. The person answering your call is limited in how much information they can provide you as they may only relate general advice. They are not able to develop a full understanding of your individual situation and they can't provide you with personal advice tailored to your specific needs. But they can help you to understand what's going on with your superannuation and what your options are.

There's no avoiding it. If you're a woman and single, it's very important for you to take ownership of your financial position and understand it. It's also important to find someone you can trust and listen to their advice.

Women seem particularly vulnerable to picking up slivers of information, and thinking they are right and the rest of the world is wrong. For example, a potential client who owned a number of small commercial properties came to see me. She had held them for several years. When she first bought them, she thought owning them was fun and a pleasant distraction. She eventually became president of the body corporate group connected to the local shopping centre in which she owned the commercial properties. Several years down the track, she was complaining she was sick of them.

If you're a woman and single, it's very important for you to take ownership of your financial position and understand it.

She'd had a couple of bad tenants and with them some bad debts and there had been a few big falling outs within the corporate body she oversaw. I suggested she sell the properties and do something more sensible with the money. She assured me she had tried to sell them but could not get her price. This is a pleasant way of saying she was asking too much for them. She was sure she was asking the right price and felt the real estate agent was trying to get the price down so he could get a mate to buy them cheaply.

She had an argument against every suggestion I made and was sure she knew better. Yet there she was sitting on an investment — her only source of income — that was continually causing her stress, was underperforming in terms of the income it was generating and which she could never rely on to sustain her through retirement. Women often fall into this trap.

There is no point seeking the advice of your accountant or your financial planner if all you are going to do is ignore their advice and tell them you know better.

And don't ask a real estate agent to value a property if you don't believe they are acting in your best interest — and being honest — by telling you the property won't sell because your price is too high. If you don't believe them, call other agents until you find one you do trust.

However, if you have spoken to five or six real estate agents and they are all telling you the same thing about a property and you feel they don't know what they are talking about, that should be a red flag. Perhaps you need to step back and have another take on the situation. It's always disappointing when an investment doesn't perform as well as you would like, but it's foolish to cling to the mistaken belief an investment is good and it's just your adviser who doesn't understand.

While I am sure there are men who suffer from this as well, it does seem to afflict women more than men. Whether women feel particularly vulnerable on their own and so become overtly defensive, or whether it's that once they commit to an investment idea they find it impossible to let go, this is a big mistake and it's something all women need to guard against. The best investment strategies are the simplest ones. The best strategies are the ones you understand and that free you to get on with enjoying your life. If the underlying investment, for whatever reason, starts taking up your time and causing you stress or concern, this is a strong indicator you should get out of it.

Make sure you understand where your money is invested

Another common mistake made by women, and to a lesser degree men, is they are reluctant to drill down to learn where their money is and why it's being invested as it is. I think at the base of this is a fear they may look ignorant.

Investing money can seem complicated and the rules surrounding superannuation in Australia are absolutely complex, so you should never feel self-conscious in asking questions about how superannuation works or where your money is invested.

In fact, if your financial planner is reluctant to spend much time explaining these issues to you, this may be a good indicator you should find another financial planner who will spend time making sure you understand.

Reading investment books such as this one helps too. Trying to keep abreast of some of the more general information provided in newspapers and radio programs is another good idea.

This learning curve doesn't need to go on forever. Once you feel confident you understand the basics in terms of where your funds are invested, you can invest those funds and leave it to your financial planner to manage the day-to-day issues around those investments.

But you should never feel you don't understand where your funds are invested or how they might be impacted by, say, a downturn in the market or a sudden rise in the value of the Australian dollar. You should at least have a general understanding of your investments. If you do, you won't be too concerned about the day-to-day movements in the value of your investments. Any investment you make in retirement should be made with a five-year time frame in mind and you shouldn't be unnerved by changes in, say, a company's share price or what you hear on the nightly news.

As you move towards retirement, you should not have your money in any investment that has even the slightest risk of going bust and leaving you penniless. If you are checking your investments on a daily basis, perhaps this is what is driving your concerns. Perhaps you are fearful of losing your money entirely. In fact, this can be a very good question to ask when an investment strategy is being put forward: 'How likely am I to lose my money in this?' If there is even the slightest possibility of losing any money, then this is the wrong investment for you in retirement.

Going it alone

Going it alone can be the hardest thing in retirement. And sadly, more and more older Australians who divorce — commonly referred to as silver splitters — are among those who find themselves in this situation. Through divorce or death, through choice or not, the reality is 25 per cent, 2.3 million, of Australian households have just one person living in them.

This makes it doubly important for you to think through your retirement plans and prepare for whatever eventualities might come your way. If you are living alone, you need to review your living arrangements. While men are faced with this issue too, in my experience they seem less sentimental and less attached to the family home. You might be desperate to stay in your family home where you feel surrounded and comforted by loving memories, but is this practical? Can you do all the tasks required to maintain the property and, if the answer is no, will you have the finances to pay for someone else to maintain your home?

Think through what would happen if you fell ill during your retirement and had to recuperate at home. When my parents retired about 40 years ago, if you were sick in retirement you would most likely suffer a slow, downward and usually irreversible deterioration of health. That isn't the case these days.

I have seen clients go through quite dire medical circumstances only to see them 12 months later looking better than they ever did before. Typically, this is because there is nothing like a health scare to prompt you to give up the cigarettes, cut back on your intake of alcohol and lose a bit of weight. Add to this a bit of mandatory exercise and most people start feeling better than they have in years.

You need to plan for this. It's likely that at some stage you will spend time in hospital and come back to your home, where community support staff will help provide care for you and where you can fully recover. You need to have a home that can accommodate this scenario. If your home has poor access or a lot of stairs, for instance, this probably isn't a good place for you to live in retirement.

Another important issue is to think through what you will do if you are no longer able to make decisions about your finances or medical care. You need to be proactive in putting in place powers of attorney — both financial and medical — so someone who cares about you can step in and make these decisions for you. It is important you write down what you would like done in these situations and to do this well ahead of time, so the message is clear and coherent.

Simplify your life

In coming to terms with possibly being alone for the rest of your life — and that's not necessarily a bad thing — you should look to simplify your life. And to be honest, most people find this one single step very liberating.

While this can apply to men, I believe it applies more commonly to women. For reasons unknown, they just seem to thrive on complicating their lives! Start with your home. A garage sale and spring clean is always a good thing and never more so than when you retire. What you can't sell, you should give away to charity or a local recycling depot and what can't be reused, you need to take to the tip. You have to be practical.

There will be times in your retirement when you can expect to need home help. Someone to come in and clean or perhaps help you recover from a minor medical event or provide some home nursing. Do your bit by making sure your home is tidy and free from clutter. Local governments are offering more and more services to help people stay in their own home, but they will observe your living conditions and have the power to recommend that you move if it seems you aren't coping with living on your own.

And while you're tidying up your home, you should also be tidying up your financial affairs. Have all your investments formally detailed in writing and keep these records in one location. If possible, store them online. Everything should be simple and clear cut.

Have a credit card for convenience, but be meticulous in paying it off in full each month.

Most people only need to have one bank account, and this should be where money comes in from your investments each month and from where all your expenses are paid each month. Have a credit card for convenience, but be meticulous in paying it off in full each month. You would be surprised how many people, even in retirement, don't. Use a credit card to make regular payments such as electricity, gas and other essential services. This can make life a lot easier as you only have to make one payment a month to keep everything ticking over.

This can be particularly useful if you have to spend time in hospital, for example. Not only will you not miss paying these bills, but you will only have to remember to make one payment a month and you can set this up to happen automatically. Everything should be simple and stress free.

Take time to sort out your paperwork. It should be easy for someone going into your home to work out where your key documents are, such as your will, medical insurance, details of your investments and titles for any properties you own.

If your finances are sorted and simplified in retirement, you should not need to lodge a tax return each year, but if this is not the case and you do need to lodge one, make sure you keep all your papers in one spot and that these are easy to sort through. Your affairs should be simplified so your tax return is much the same year after year and the papers you need to complete it are easy to find.

Sexually transmitted debt

When I started out as a journalist in the early 1980s, 'sexually transmitted debt' was a catchy headline that sent readers off giggling about its double entendre. It might sound a bit passé to use the term these days, but unfortunately this type of debt still exists. Sexually transmitted debt is debt held in your name as the result of your relationship with someone.

Typically it happens when a woman has been on her own for a while and suddenly finds herself in a relationship — and I say that only because in these situations you might find your defences are a bit lower than normal. It can start off simply enough. Your partner needs to borrow money to replace a car or to go travelling with you and for whatever reasons they can't access normal lines of credit so they call on you to lend them money.

It can end in quite extreme situations. For example, I had a client who came to see me with her new partner. He had lots of great ideas for their new future together. They were going to sell her home, which she had steadily paid off over the previous 10 years and which she was fond of. They were going to draw down her super savings and combine them with the proceeds from selling her house to buy a new property from which they were going to run B&B-style holiday accommodation. Soon after buying their new home, it became obvious they had to do a number of renovations on the property to stay competitive in the rather fickle world of short-term accommodation providers, so a mortgage was quickly put over the property.

As part of this strategy, she was going to stop working at a job she loved and run the B&B full time. Until this new project was bedded down and profitable, he was to keep working, keep his superannuation intact and keep a property he owned in Melbourne as it was negatively geared against his income. Sweet. All except for the fact that a year or so into this new lifestyle a few things became apparent. She didn't like spending most of her time cleaning up after other people in the B&B and she felt she was shouldering an unfair burden of the new business.

The business proved much harder to manage than they had anticipated, and they hadn't expected to receive the comments being left about the property on Tripadvisor and the adverse impact they had on the business. These troubles prompted a lot of domestic disharmony and the relationship ended when he found someone new to live with. He walked away with his well-paying job intact, and his super savings greatly enhanced because he had been living rent free for a few years so he was able to increase his super contributions. He was also able to maximise the advantages of renting out his property in Melbourne.

In contrast, she had left her job as a teacher, which she had enjoyed a lot more than cleaning a B&B and was unable to return to it. She found the stress of running the B&B by herself intolerable and quickly closed it. She then found herself with no income, no superannuation and a mortgage on the property she couldn't afford.

Now that's an extreme case, but so often that's how these things work out. Somehow it is the chap always coming up with the bright ideas for creating a new future and, somehow, he walks away better off financially — win, lose or draw. It just seems the way of the world.

That's not to say you shouldn't plan a new future together if you find someone special, but you should always leave the door open and have an exit strategy in case things don't work out, particularly if you are planning a new life based around a new partner.

Online scamming

Online scamming is a modern-day thing that has taken on a life of its own. It is based on the pervasive presence of the internet and the way all of us can find ourselves online alone, late at night, often after having had a few glasses of wine. We are at our most vulnerable. Online scammers are very much alive and sadly women seem to be more likely to become victims to them than men. But having said that, men can be vulnerable to being exploited too.

There are all sorts of online scammers. There are the invoices for bogus goods that suddenly appear in your email inbox, sent in the hope you are an honest person who pays all their bills. In the flurry of modern life you think you forgot to pay and don't take the time to check if this is actually money you owe. You pay the invoice almost automatically. And once the money is sent, it's gone.

Then there are the more elaborate scams. We are all aware of the classic Nigerian scammer who asks you to send money in order for them to pay the lawyers who will then release the assets of an estate that has been left to them, or money that will allow them to claim an unclaimed winning lottery ticket. As surprising as it might sound, according to ASIC these scams are still successful and people fall for them despite all the negative publicity they have attracted over the years.

Scammers come in all shapes and sizes. There are the online threats to your life if you don't pay the person scamming you. There are remote access scams where the perpetrator will demand you buy software from them in order to stop them sending a virus to your computer or software. There are phishing and identity-theft scammers who try to access your bank accounts and steal money directly from them.

The most worrying scammers are those who arrive via online dating sites. Worrying because these scammers can get past their victims' best defences by bringing you into their world, telling you what you want to hear, and claiming they care for you and you will live happily ever after as soon as you send them some money. These scammers are most worrying because the scams can go on for years. Typically, they will start out small, asking for relatively modest amounts, but invariably the requests come for ever-increasing amounts of money. The stories behind why they need the money from you also become bigger.

By the time you realise something is wrong, you may have sent them tens of thousands of dollars, if not more, and you might be left too embarrassed to report the matter. ASIC claims more than $1.7 million has been lost by Australians caught up in online dating scams and older Australians seem to be more vulnerable than younger Australians to this type of scamming.

The fact many retirees in Australia now have access to significant retirement savings makes them easy pickings on the world stage for online scammers. The hard facts are, never give money to anyone you have only met over the internet and be careful about giving money to anyone who has recently entered your life. Your retirement savings are there to support you throughout what may be a very long retirement and giving away large chunks of it early in your retirement is a sure-fire way of ruining any chances of that.

Put yourself first

This is where women, particularly those living by themselves, just have to lift their game; there's no other way of putting it. One of the things that make women so special is they are caring, nurturing and happy to put the interests of others ahead of their own. It is largely what helps the world go round. While this is an admirable quality in relation to most things, it's not a good attitude to have regarding your finances, especially when it comes to planning your retirement.

As the 2016 federal Senate report showed, the consequences of women not taking control of their finances can lead to homelessness and prolonged periods of poverty and uncertainty. All at a time in their lives when they are at their most vulnerable. And the only person who can change this is you. Even if you have never taken control of your finances before, retirement is the time when you must step up and do this.

That's not to say you have to spend every hour of every week worrying about your financial situation. Far from it. However, you should find a good adviser you feel comfortable with to talk to as soon as retirement appears on your distant horizon. Take stock of your situation when you still have time to boost your retirement savings and boost them significantly.

Once you are about to retire you need to have another serious conversation with your financial planner about how your funds are going to be invested and how these investments are going to generate an income for you in retirement. As I've mentioned, you need to insist your planner explains these investments in a way you can understand and if they can't, find another financial planner who can clearly explain their proposed investment options to you.

In retirement you need to live within your means as there is no going back.

Once you've had that conversation, you should have a clear idea of exactly how much money you will have to live on, including any Age Pension entitlements. This is important because retirement is all about living off the income being generated by your investments and staying within this fixed income.

If you've never been good at living on a budget, now is the time to learn. If this is a problem, you will need to re-think some of your expenditure as you move into retirement. Alternatively, you might need to think about generating additional sources of funds.

Either way, in retirement you need to live within your means as there is no going back. The key to having a long, happy and financially successful retirement is making sure the amount you are spending each year is less than the income being generated by your investments.

Oh, and remember to enjoy life

Sometimes I think in the hustle and bustle of being a financial planner I don't talk enough to clients about the non-financial aspects of their retirement. And that's a shame as retirement can be the most exciting stage of your life if you open yourself to the endless possibilities it can offer. This is particularly the case for women.

This is a time for sitting down and thinking about the things that excite you in life and capture your imagination. The answer will be different for everyone, and so it should be. Life should not be restricted by money.

I know of a successful writer who reached retirement life and found she had almost no retirement savings, which is often the case for women working in creative areas. Limited to life on the Age Pension, she made a couple of brave decisions. She tidied up her house and made it as presentable as possible and rented it out for short periods of time, mainly to friends of friends and mostly on mates' rates in the hope they would look after it a bit better than if it was on a more normal tenancy.

Then she looked around to find countries that had favourable exchange rates with Australia and tracked down cheap airfares to travel to them. Once there, she would spend several weeks cycling around, exploring the countryside. Not only did she keep the costs down to a minimum, but she got fit at the same time. She found the exchange rate was so favourable that her pension dollars went much further for her overseas than in Australia.

There are lots of exciting things you can turn your hand to. Australia is alive with local clubs and activity groups. You can get involved in practically anything you dream of — from volunteer acting groups to sailing on boats at your local yacht club. None of these things require much in the way of money either, so it can be possible to live an active life and still remain within a budget.

There are hiking clubs and bird watching clubs and bike riding clubs. I've even noticed in my local shopping centre they have put together a walking group for local older citizens to come on indoor walking tours of the centre before and after trading hours. It might seem a bit odd, but it provides older Australians with a completely safe, weather-proof environment for walking where there is a slip-free surface friendly to anyone requiring a walking stick or frame to get around.

While retirement can be tough on men, it can be particularly hard on women. They can find themselves widowed or divorced and living very lonely lives, but only if they choose to. Just as you need to seek out companionship, so others may seek you out as a possible companion. What's more, the statistics are clear. People who lead active lives involved with their local groups and volunteering not only live longer lives, they live healthier lives. They stay mentally aware for longer. Typically, they are able to stay in their own homes longer and live active lives for longer. It's a great win–win.

So, remember to ...

- *take good care of yourself.* A lot of the information in this chapter is directed to women but it can equally apply to men. In fact, it really applies to anyone who feels a bit lost, a bit alone and a bit concerned that they have left planning for their retirement too late.

- *understand where your money is invested.* If you feel uncertain about your financial position, you need to make more of an effort to understand where your money is invested and make sure you are getting the best possible advice. It can be tough if you don't have someone you trust to bounce ideas off, but you still need to be diligent.

- *simplify your life.* This involves everything from your domestic situation to the way you manage your finances. If there is only you to look after things, make life as easy as you can for yourself.

- *keep money separate from your love life.* It can be easy as we get older to think we know what we're doing and that we are good judges of other people. That may or may not be the case. Regardless, when it comes to your precious retirement savings, keep them completely separate from that special person in your life.

- *stay safe online.* Being alone makes everyone just that little bit more vulnerable and more willing to believe something or someone when they shouldn't. There are scammers everywhere these days and both men and women can be vulnerable to being taken advantage of. Take care when dealing with people online.

- *put yourself first.* If there is no-one in your life to make you feel special, then you need to take extra steps to make yourself feel special. Be positive and optimistic. You never know who or what might be just around the corner. In the meantime, take the time to be kind to yourself and treat yourself occasionally.

Take a moment to ...

... write down all the ways you would like someone to spoil you if you had someone special in your life.

Keep this list in reserve. Then, when you come across those moments when you're a bit down, pull it out and make sure you spoil yourself. In fact, why not make a day of spoiling yourself a regular feature of your life?

_____

_____

_____

_____

_____

_____

Chapter 9
Build your escape hatch

Despite the best planning in the world, stuff can happen. With retirement stretching for 30 years or more, you need to expect to suffer a few financial or physical setbacks. It's called life.

The best defences are to get good advice from the outset, so you avoid the bigger financial mistakes, and to plan for the occasional adverse event, so if things go wrong, you can calmly say, 'I thought this might happen and this is how I am going to react'. Taking some simple steps will help.

Understand what the problem is that you are facing. Is it a short-term issue that will right itself if you're patient and don't panic, or is it something significant and permanent that you're going to have to take major steps to correct? You might find during your retirement, the share market takes a major step down and drags down the value of your investments with it. This can be a terrible experience, particularly if you are relatively inexperienced in investing.

By choosing safe, secure investments at the outset, you should be protected. Yes, the value of these assets might fall during a downturn but they should recover with time. This was the case during the GFC in 2008–09, where the value of even the best companies in Australia drifted down during 2008 and 2009 but by 2010 most had returned to where they were before the GFC.

Don't panic. Typically, people who say they lost thousands of dollars during the GFC had either invested poorly to begin with or panicked and sold good assets as the market was falling, or both. This effectively locks in those losses and denies you the chance of riding the market back up in the eventual recovery that follows any downturn.

People convince themselves the good times will roll on forever and that they won't be impacted by any downward movements in the investment markets or the economy generally. When they find they are wrong, they panic, sell and lock in their losses, which is not the way to go. There will always be ups and downs when it comes to investing and while you shouldn't talk yourself into being too nervous about what might happen in the future, you shouldn't ignore the fact that downturns in the market do occur.

If you step back from investment markets you can get a better perspective on them and be better prepared for any downturns when they happen. Be vigilant of changes as they appear on the horizon and modify your investments and perhaps your spending accordingly. A good financial planner will help you moderate your portfolio to adjust to changing conditions and ride out any sudden downturns that might come your way.

Take control

Keep an eye on your investments, especially through the early years of your retirement. There are two key factors to watch:

- Is your portfolio generating more income than you are drawing down in terms of income, fees and expenses?

- Will your portfolio steadily rise in value over the long term?

If you don't believe the income being generated is covering all the outgoings, take steps to fix this. Ignoring the situation will make it worse, as the shortfall in income will steadily erode the capital that is available to generate the income. The less capital, the less income being generated, meaning more capital is being distributed to you by way of income, meaning even less capital is available to generate income.

It's also important to determine whether this is a short-term event or whether you have miscalculated how much you are spending and there is a structural problem in the way you have set things up.

If it becomes clear you have permanently miscalculated how much money you need in retirement, then you need to revisit your retirement plans completely. You might have to face up to some hard decisions that you have been putting off since you retired. For example, maybe it was foolhardy to think you could keep a holiday home in retirement. Now you've stopped working and are trying to live on a fixed income, you might see this won't be possible. Alternatively, you might realise while you once thought staying in the family home was the best choice for you, that's no longer realistic and you should move to something smaller and more affordable.

There are also two other options:

- *You can look at your investment choices.* Are you making your money work hard enough? At the start of retirement you may have been so concerned about security that you put all your retirement savings into term deposits and are now paying the consequence of that decision by finding you don't have sufficient funds to live on. If that's the case, you may need to reconsider. This can be a difficult area for retirees because in chasing higher returns on investments you will be taking on more risk. You need to be mindful of this and not chase higher returns without thinking about the inevitable risk you are taking on.

- *You can tighten your belt and reduce your expenditure.* If you act early, it may only take a year or two of cutting back to bring your portfolio back into equilibrium and nothing more drastic needs to be done. Of course, it could always take longer.

Seek advice

If things do go wrong in retirement, seek good advice. That might be hard to do if the reason things have gone wrong is due to your financial planner not having provided you with good advice. Finding a new financial planner might be hard, but it's an important move. They will be able to give you a frank assessment of your current financial situation and just how bad things are as well as whether you are likely to recover. That's important information and it's information you're unlikely to get from the person who put you into the failed investment. Typically, they will be covering their tracks and putting the best light they can on the situation.

A new financial planner will also be able to outline a way forward so this time make sure you understand where your money is invested.

Your new financial planner will be able to advise whether you have a case against your previous adviser and what you should do about it. Typically, they won't get involved themselves, but they should be able to provide details of the financial services ombudsman's office, which may be able to act on your behalf. All financial planners belong to a complaints resolution scheme so you should find out which scheme your previous adviser belongs to and work from there.

Although losing money is always a worry, keeping your emotions under control is the key to getting a reasonable resolution, particularly if you believe the person who talked you into making the investment is at fault.

In fact, this is the one time in your life when you need to stay very cold and considered. Collect all the documentation you can about the investment that has gone bad and try to construct a timeline from when the investment was first put before you. Ideally, you will have kept clear records of every conversation you had with the promoter of the investment and if your records are patchy, then piece together as well as you can how you believe you were persuaded into making the investment. The quality and detail of this information will probably be the biggest single determiner of whether you get any money back.

Re-evaluate your situation

Given you may spend several decades in retirement, it is reasonable to expect there will be financial setbacks along the way. Stay calm and re-evaluate your situation.

It's unlikely to be as bad as it first appears. If you experienced financial loss in the early years of retirement and it is a significant loss, you need to think of ways to rebuild your investments. There are options. You might need to restructure your financial affairs or take another look at what you want to achieve in retirement. If you are able to return to the workforce, then rebuilding your superannuation savings might be an option.

The legendary Bart Cummings had set himself up for a long and happy retirement. Just as he was about to step back from racing for good, disaster struck and he was declared bankrupt. Something few people know is Bart Cummings trained more Melbourne Cup winners after he retired then he did during his long, illustrious career prior to 'retirement'. He also went on to build a close and successful business relationship with one of his grandsons, which could only have been a delight to him as he grew older. So you can recover from even the hardest setbacks.

Remain positive

Most first meetings I have with prospective clients follow much the same pattern. They outline their hopes for retirement, then their assets and then they look a bit grim. Relax, I always say. Retirement is a good news story in Australia. Hopefully, you will find retirement is the happiest time in your lives.

This is still the case even if things go wrong. There are situations where due to either lack of good planning or where good planning has not been enough, everything has gone badly. You've made an investment, or even been advised to make an investment, and it all goes wrong and ends up worthless or at least worth significantly less than what you bought it for.

It's all about coming to terms with investing funds and living off the income they generate.

Don't let financial setbacks overwhelm you in retirement. It's easy to be overcome with embarrassment because at a time in your life when you believe you should know better, you've made a bad investment or been misguided by a bad adviser and lost money. It can be a body blow if you let it — so don't let it.

I know I've said it before, but Australia is blessed with a great social security system and a generous Age Pension. It's a fantastic safety net if things go badly in terms of your investments in retirement. It's also backed up by a first-rate medical system. No matter what you think at first glance, no matter what happens to your financial investments, it's not as bad as you think.

It's all about coming to terms with investing funds and living off the income they generate. You will have good investments and good years and you will have bad investments and bad years. The fact you're retired does not magically protect you from the harsh realities of investing money. Anyone who has invested money successfully has also lost money from investing.

Try to avoid the biggest pitfalls in retirement. For example, if you are fortunate enough to reach retirement and own your own home, whatever you do don't let yourself be talked into borrowing against it. This can lead to big problems down the track that can be difficult to recover from.

You'll recall in chapter 4 I talked about the failed Storm Financial group. I was horror-struck when I heard about Storm's clients and the devastating losses inflicted on them by the poor advice of its financial planners. It must have been a truly terrible experience for everyone involved. Yet these clients have mostly moved on with life and made the most of their situations. The most important defence you have in these situations is your state of mind and refusing to let setbacks, no matter how devastating they are at the time, hold you down.

Review your back-up plan

Many people retire and decide to manage their own financial affairs. They do all the right things: learn about investments, act conscientiously and manage their money effectively. That's great as long as they are fit and able to keep doing this. However, there are two downsides to this you need to keep in mind:

- Typically in these situations, there is only one partner who is interested in managing the couple's financial affairs. They're the one who knows where all the paperwork is, meets with the accountant every year and makes all the investment decisions. They see no reason to employ a financial planner or in fact to tell anyone what they are doing. They have it all under control, and fair enough. If you're happy and interested enough to take control of your financial affairs, that's great. All the more power to you. Sadly, these situations can end in tears if the partner who looks after the financial affairs becomes ill, or sadder still, passes on. This can leave the surviving partner with an enormous headache at a time in their life when they are least able to cope with it because they are dealing with medical issues and bills or coming to terms with the fact their partner isn't coming back. Inevitably they let things drift. What was well ordered and under control steadily descends into chaos and it can be difficult at this point to put together what is going on financially.

- As you move through retirement, your attitude to managing money changes. While you may have happily spent a morning a month or perhaps every week looking after your financial affairs, as you grow older this will not be the case. Typically as you progress through your eighties and nineties you will be less interested in money and will generally spend less. There will be less to manage and you will be increasingly distracted by other things in your life. In addition, it is most likely you will not be as sharp or as mobile as you once were and both of these things will work against you managing your affairs effectively.

If you don't want to employ a financial planner, at least find someone you know and trust and bring them up to speed with your financial situation. Then if something happens to you, your partner will at least know there's someone they can turn to who you had confidence in. This isn't ideal as even the most devoted family member has their own life to live and their own financial affairs to look after. There is also the reality that you are putting a lot of trust into someone who may be tempted to put your best interests second to theirs at some point down the track.

I suggest that if you start losing interest in managing your affairs, proactively move the day-to-day management of your assets to a reputable financial planner and remain heavily involved with what is happening with your investments. It's not a sign of defeat. It's a sign of good planning. At least this way if something happens to you, your funds will be looked after.

Staying in your own home

Most Australians hope to stay in their own home for as long as possible in retirement and that's an admirable goal and something to strive towards. It shouldn't blind you to the fact your life might be much improved by moving into a retirement home. Many facilities have a wide raft of activities and support groups and you might find you enjoy life more fully by moving into a home. If you are determined to stay in your own home for as long as you can, think it through.

Ensure your home is reasonable in terms of the accommodation it provides. It needs to be well maintained and practical. A two-storey home is always going to be problematic because most people find as they get older their ability to negotiate steps becomes harder. It also needs to be relatively close to services and public transport, otherwise you are going to face significant problems moving around as you will stop driving at some point.

The federal government has made it clear it is supportive of people staying in their own homes for as long as possible and there are local community initiatives to help ensure this happens. These services can extend the length of time you stay in your own home significantly. Make sure you set yourself up to take full advantage of them. Your home needs to be relatively modern in terms of the kitchen and bathrooms and it needs to have easy access so you can still move around once you start losing mobility.

While this might not be important during the early stages of retirement it will be later. Your family home may have suited you perfectly during the first 10 years of retirement, but it may not be up to scratch after that.

It doesn't have to cost a lot to age-proof your home. For example, you could:

- improve the lighting in entranceways and outdoor areas

- replace doorknobs with lever handles, which are easier to manipulate

- install bathroom grab bars and raised toilet seats

- get rid of scatter rugs and attach colourful traction strips to the front edge of your stairs to help prevent falls.

None of these changes costs much money.

Another benefit for those wanting to stay at home are virtual retirement villages, which are starting to spring up on the internet. These can help seniors access resources to make it easier to stay in their home for longer. A virtual village is a local, non-profit organisation that posts information online, providing referrals to member-recommended service companies and volunteers — for example, to help out with dog walking, yard work and other homeowner needs.

Aged care options

While we are all living longer, we may not be able to proactively care for and look after ourselves in later years. There are a million physical issues that can beset you as you grow older and just as many psychological problems, such as dementia, that can stop even the most determined retiree from remaining at home. Like all things, the more planning you do ahead of time, the better the outcome.

Aged care facilities enable you to live out your final days with dignity and enjoyment. A lot of people find living in an aged care facility can be a big step up in terms of having more people in their lives and more social interaction — and at the end of the day, we are all social creatures.

The options available in the way of aged care facilities are almost endless — and prices can vary significantly so shop around. You also need to choose carefully as there are good and bad facilities out there. If you are looking at buying into an aged care facility, you need to find a caring solicitor who specialises in this area and have them advise you as to the pros and cons of making this type of investment.

Most likely you will have to sell your home. There should be some spare funds left over to help provide for you and to leave to your beneficiaries. These are things you will just have to get your mind around. You need to be proactive and find an aged care facility that offers you a price and contractual terms that you're comfortable with.

If you are not proactive about investigating your options, these decisions will be made for you later in life and they are unlikely to be ones you like. Typically, it will be because you have been admitted to hospital and the hospital is pressuring your family to find an aged care facility for you. Their choice will most likely be dominated by where they can quickly find a bed.

If you are proactive you can usually manage the situation better than this. You should be able to buy into a facility that will offer you supported living in your own villa or apartment. If down the track you suffer an adverse medical condition, then typically they will find a supported bed within their own facility. It can take a lot of strain off your family to investigate the facilities that are close to you and, importantly, close to your family if you hope to see them during the later stages of your life.

Funeral plan options

In planning to fully fund your final years, it is reasonable to include paying for your funeral, although I don't know of any other subject that polarises clients as quickly as this one. Some clients believe adamantly this is something their children can take care of, while others are adamant they don't want their children wasting money on this ceremony.

It is worth mentioning some of the pros and cons of funeral bonds. This can be something to think about if you are trying to qualify — or have qualified — for an Age Pension and you want to boost your benefits.

The federal government offers an incentive to encourage all Australians to take out funeral bonds. At the time of writing, by contributing $12 750 into an approved funeral bond, and decreasing your accessible assets by this amount, you could boost your Age Pension entitlements by $994.50 a year for a single pensioner or $1989 a year for a couple. By making this one, simple investment, you can achieve an after-tax return of 7.8 per cent net guaranteed. That's the sort of return I like.

If the level of your assets is such that you won't qualify for the Age Pension, you might be indecisive about the need to take out a funeral bond. A lot of people dislike them because they basically take your money and lock it up until you die, at which point the funds may or may not be sufficient to pay for your funeral. As a result, a lot of people prefer to keep their funds to themselves, invest them effectively and wind up with more money in their estate to pay for their funeral. In addition, some funeral bonds are set up so you effectively pay more into them over many years than you will ever receive. Make sure you read the fine print and obtain a bond that is good value. As I said, few topics polarise clients as much as this one.

So what are funeral bonds? A funeral bond is a specialised investment that enables you to put aside funds to meet future funeral expenses. You can do this by way of a regular savings scheme or a lump sum payment.

An investment in a funeral bond is similar to putting money into a trust account that can accrue interest and becomes payable at the time of death. The benefits can only be used to meet your funeral expenses and once these are paid any remaining funds usually revert back to the company providing the bonds.

No two funeral bonds are the same, but most have the following features:

- The money invested is as secure as the company offering the bond. Typically, they provide for you to choose your own funeral director and you generally plan the size of the funeral by deciding how much money you want to put into the funeral bond.

- Most funeral bonds don't guarantee to cover the cost of your funeral; they simply guarantee to contribute a pre-agreed amount to your funeral. As a result, it is quite possible inflation will mean the cost of your funeral exceeds the amount you have put towards it.

The biggest plus of putting money into funeral bonds is that Centrelink exempts funeral bonds from both the assets and income tests.

Estate planning

If you've successfully structured your retirement so your finances will last as long as you do, you need to make sure you put in place an effective will. If you don't do this and die intestate — that is, without a will — the State Trustees' office in your state will step in and administer your estate according to some fairly stringent laws and charge your estate a fee for doing so. Not only can this be an expensive option in terms of your estate, but it may also lead to your assets being distributed to people you would rather not have receive them.

This issue is particularly important if you have a blended family or children from several relationships. It can be a minefield of legal complexities, and litigation over deceased estates has literally exploded in recent years. Once upon a time an average couple might have left behind a modest house in the suburbs and maybe a few term deposits. The explosion in house prices in even modest suburbs in Australia's capital cities combined with the advent of superannuation, where couples can have hundreds of thousands of dollars tucked away in retirement savings, means even families that would have thought themselves very average in terms of their financial circumstances leave behind significant estates.

The size of these estates means it is worthwhile for solicitors to dispute the content of wills because they will be paid from the estate for their services. The larger the estate, the more certain these lawyers can be of achieving success for their clients and also of being paid.

The best way to head this off is to ensure you find a caring solicitor who can spend time with you to draft a valid will to protect your estate from these sorts of unwanted legal contests. This won't come cheap. You will need to spend several thousand dollars — more if you have a particularly large estate or if your wishes are particularly complex. However, it is money well spent.

While you are visiting with your solicitor, make sure you put in place valid powers of attorney, both medical and financial. Have clear documentation in place regarding any future medical requirements you might have and whether, for example, you would like a DNR order (an order instructing health care providers not to perform CPR if your breathing stops or if your heart stops beating) put in place. Again, this will save your family unnecessary stress at a time when they can least deal with the impact of not having these important documents in place.

In addition to these powerful documents you should write what is now referred to as a living will. This is an informal letter written by you about any issue you think is important that you think might be beneficial to clarify a situation. Typically, a living will details the sort of funeral arrangements you would like and whether there are any specific family mementos you would like passed on to individual people. While a living will is not legally binding, it can go a long way towards answering questions that your loved ones might be faced with after you're gone.

It is also important to keep your will up to date. Sadly, it is possible as you grow older that you will not see your children as much as you might like and that other people — neighbours or friends — might step in and shoulder caring for you in your final years. You might feel the need to provide for these people. Make sure you do so formally and that any new will you execute is clearly witnessed. You should make your intentions known to your other beneficiaries, usually your children, so there is no dispute or disagreement about your wishes. If you don't do this formally by writing a legally binding will, at least make sure you make mention of it in your living will. The clearer your intentions, the less likely it is that your estate will be disputed and precious funds wasted on legal fees spent trying to resolve the situation.

So, remember to ...

- *take control of your financial situation*. Many retirees just let their superannuation savings sit there without an investment strategy. They draw down funds when and as they need to. Don't do this. Have an investment strategy in place and stick to it.

- *accept there will be ups and downs*. Keep these events in perspective and don't panic. If you've been sensible with your investment choices, any downturn should be short lived and have little long-term impact.

- *remain positive*. Don't panic and assume that a downturn will continue forever. All investment markets have their cycles and they will recover with time. If you're not confident investing large sums of money, then make sure you engage a caring adviser to help you.

- *stay independent for as long as you can*. Don't rush into the next stage of retirement, whatever you perceive that to be. Focus on living independently for as long as you can and set yourself up so your surroundings help you achieve that goal.

- *be positive if you need to move into a retirement home.* Often clients experience a real boost when they move into a retirement home. Free from the hassle of doing everything yourself at home and surrounded by a new group of people much the same age as yourself, you can enjoy a whole new lease on life.

- *get your affairs in order.* Make sure you take the time to keep your will up to date and ensure it reflects your current intentions because these may change as you grow older. Think about taking out a funeral plan, but be careful to read through the fine print to ensure you don't pay in more than you will receive.

Take a moment to ...

... take control of your future.

Write down the key steps you need to take as you move into retirement and tick each one off as you complete it.

_____

_____

_____

_____

_____

_____

A final word

I hope I have encouraged you to be more optimistic about what you are able to achieve in retirement and that something, somewhere in this book prompts you to rethink your plans and create a wonderful future for yourself.

I know it's easy to dismiss these suggestions and be pessimistic. 'What would she know?', I hear you say. 'She's probably had a privileged life, living overseas on a wealthy expatriate allowance, where she's made a lot of money, and come back to Australia to live the good life.'

Some of that is true, but like most people I have had my ups and downs. Both my parents have passed on and, sadly, I lost two beautiful babies, although happily they have been survived by three adorable boys. I have been through an acrimonious divorce and I have had a serious brush with cancer.

All of this makes me very much like the people I suspect will read this book.

Every bad event in life is like a body blow. It stops you in your tracks. It takes your breath away. It can take quite a while to recover. Sometimes people don't recover. That, though, is the challenge in life. To get up and start again.

If you take nothing else away from this book, I hope you will focus on the following thoughts:

- *Take your time.* Retirement can last a long time. Consider all your options and try to think outside the square. The possibilities of what you can do are endless.

- *Don't stress too much.* While it is easy to believe you don't have enough money set aside for retirement, this is unlikely. Australia's first-rate social security system and Age Pension provide a valuable safety net for everyone.

- *Keep your finances simple.* If you don't fully understand where your money is being invested and what sort of income it will generate for you, then don't invest your precious retirement savings there. Choose an investment option you do understand.

- *Get good advice.* This is important in the lead-up to retirement as well as when you stop working. Make sure you take advantage of every opportunity to boost your retirement savings and then to maximise your retirement income.

- *Enjoy your life.* If you have made good choices and invested your savings in solid, reliable, income-generating investments, the only thing left to do is enjoy your retirement. Don't miss out on that opportunity.

If you think you would like to start a conversation with me, specifically about your retirement plans, I am always happy to discuss your situation. Please don't hesitate to contact me:

Email: patricia@patriciahoward.com.au
Website: www.patriciahoward.com.au

Patricia Howard

Index

bill payment, automatic 144
blog, starting a 108–9
book, writing a 107–8
boom-and-bust cycle,
    Australian 45
bottom line, knowing 93–4
'bucket list' items 95–6
budgeting 16–17
  — apps for 93–4
  — in retirement 36–7
business
  — actual value of 4–5
  — funding retirement by
    selling 125–6
  — helping children buy or
    start 126–7
  — passing on 124–6
  — starting 102–4
business premises, owning 125
'buy low and sell high' rule 54

capital
  — growing through
    retirement 97
  — overspending on 94
capital gains tax (CGT) on
    property 51
capital guaranteed products 73–4
capital protected products 73–4
career, changing 6–7
Centrelink
  — assets and income tests 29–30
  — assets 'deeming rate' 31
  — assets gifting rules 31–2
  — treatment of annuities 47

children
  — helping in good ways 121–3
  — passing on a
    business to 124–6
  — paying debts of 119
  — starting or buying a
    business 126–7
clubs, local 150
co-contribution scheme for
    low-income workers 7
comfortable retirement, income for
    35–6
community involvement 113–14
complaints resolution scheme for
    financial planners 156
concessional contribution caps
    on super 12
'contracts for difference' 72–3
controlling your super 8
Costello, Peter 11
couple, home-owning, assets for
    pension 29
credit card, having for
    convenience 144
Cummings, Bart, recovering from
    setbacks 157
currency conversion, cost of 56–7
cutting back on spending 97–9

dating website scams 147
debt
  — getting rid of 23–4
  — investments with 68
  — sexually transmitted 144–6
deeming rate for assets 31